how to help your child with music

how to help your child with music

M. EMETT WILSON
Professor of Instrumental Music at Ohio State University

HENRY SCHUMAN · NEW YORK

manufactured in the united states of america
by h. wolff
designed by robert goldston

The author wishes to express his thanks to C. G. Conn, Ltd. of Elkhart, Indiana for permission to use the pictures reproduced in this book.

preface

WITH THE INTRODUCTION OF THE PHONOGRAPH and radio into all American homes, a cataclysmic change has taken place in our musical culture. We have become a musically literate people—almost overnight. Music, which used to be studied in the same formal manner in which Latin and Greek were taught, is now heard by children as often as the mother tongue. Children can learn to play music in much the same manner they learn to talk.

Which of the many instruments available should the child undertake? Which is a mere whim of today; and which will be useful when he is an adult? How long does it take to learn the instrument? What does it cost? And, most important—*what can the parent do to help the undertaking*?

The following analysis of the situation today is an attempt to help the parent find the answer to these and other questions pertaining to the musical development of the child. Children today are naturally musical. The enjoyment of music is part of their American heritage. Let us make the most of it!

M. EMETT WILSON

contents

I

before music lessons begin

Music for the untal-ented

MUSIC BEGINS AT BIRTH. BABIES HAVE ALWAYS been lulled to sleep by song or by their own crooning. Where there are many lullabies musical growth and interest is encouraged. In this day, when the crib is never far from the radio, the infant becomes as familiar with the sounds of music as with the sounds of the mother tongue. To shape these sounds into music is as easy as to shape the sounds of language into meanings.

Some children accomplish this with ease and require little help. We say they are *talented*. Others show little natural interest in the patterns of musical sound.

No one knows what talent is nor how important it is in the development of a musician. Nor should the parent be overly concerned about it. Parents will spend much more money on the child whose health is precarious than on the robust child. The same attitude should hold in music. If a child's ear is not keen, all the more reason why he should develop it. In any event no child should be left without the resource of music in a world where music plays such an increasingly important role.

Beginning

Early music training is much like early muscle training. There is no particular order in which it must be learned. A planned sequence of exercises might do more harm than good. The small child, like the child at any age, will learn fastest what he wants to use. The words the baby learns first are not necessarily the simplest ones; they are the ones connected with things in which he is interested. A small child sometimes picks up a most unusual vocabulary.

If the baby learns the easy "mama" first, it is not because it is the easiest but because it brings results. Similarly, the child will pick out first the musical sounds which are most significant to him. Much better let him make his own selection than try to force some manufactured scheme of ours on him. The order he selects will be a good order; he will learn it faster and with more enthusiasm because it is his. Music is an art dependent on feeling; as soon as we lose feeling, music is dead.

Habit

The bogey of bad habits which may be acquired during this early musical experience is a threat manufactured by music teachers who can conceive only their traditional path to musical performance. Notice how a baby grabs a teaspoon, folding his whole hand around it. He uses it this way thousands of times during the next few years. When the control and muscles of his hand have developed sufficiently to make a new manner of holding it more efficient, he suddenly shifts to the new position. Having served its purpose the old habit is dropped.

In the teaching of music a parent can hasten such a shift to more efficient position and fingering by placing the child's hand, or by calling attention to a particular twist in a certain melody that is being sung, and thus make the child's ear more critical. If the correction be forced, however, or if drill be imposed, the loss of spontaneity will offset any gain of sophisticated control.

Feeling

Music is an art; it must be felt. Especially at the beginning the feeling must be one of fun, of pleasant exploration. As soon as the idea of *ought* or *must* comes in, the interest in playing and the development of musical taste are inhibited. Compulsory drill is dangerous unless and until the child—and, for that matter, the adult—feels the need of acquiring technique.

Parents' part

Fortunately, encouraging the child's natural development is just the help the parent is best fitted to provide. It is in his baby days that a child may be determining the amount of eye-mindedness and ear-mindedness he is going to have. (The child of deaf and dumb parents does not learn to talk, unless he is brought into close association with people who can talk.) Sounds must have significance or they will not be learned. To be noticed, musical tones must bring some pleasant experience or they will not be noticed. The imitaton of a cow mooing, the cry of *peek-a-boo*, the comfortable rhyming and the satisfying rhythms of *Mother Goose*—all develop a feeling for the fundamental elements of music.

The songs a child hears in babyhood determine the melodic patterns to which he will respond, just as definitely as the words used in his presence will shape his vocabulary. And it is the songs which make an impression on the feelings that are most quickly learned. How much more quickly a child picks up the word *damn*, when exclaimed once with feeling, than colorless words used dozens of times in his presence!

The father who slapped his child hard as he held him up to look at Napoleon, saying, "Now you will never forget that you have seen Napoleon," probably carried his point. Such associations of sounds with feelings is the type of learning which a parent naturally fosters. With a little thought, he can do more for the child at this age than a formal teacher.

Singing

Singing to the child or with the child sharpens his consciousness of melodic units—melodic vocabulary. Since songs have rhythm, the rhythmic units are also developed. Rhythm can be even more enthusiastically developed in games which involve muscular action. "Patty-cake, patty-cake, baker-man" is such a rhythmic game. Marching around the table to the music of either piano or phonograph, is another way of developing a fundamental pattern of rhythm. Skipping develops more complex rhythms. "Peter, Peter, Pumpkin-Eater" or "Chopsticks" played on the piano are chiefly rhythmic experiences; the child does not learn the melody by ear but finds it by a visual pattern on the keyboard. The rhythm, however, he controls by his *feeling* for the rhythm; there is no visual pattern for that until he learns notation.

Rhythm band

The rhythm band is an effective way of developing this feeling for rhythm. The instruments which make up the rhythm band—triangle, tambourine, bell, sticks, clappers, castanets, etc.—can be bought for a few dollars. Or they can be assembled or made by a handy parent from materials on hand. And if this is done with the help of the child, all the better. The group needs a pianist to play simple tunes; this could be the parent's role. Music, with printed parts for each player, may be had. More effective is music improvised for the separate parts and taught to the separate players. In this way the teacher can suit each part to the player's ability. Having mastered the first simple version, the child will be both better able and more willing to attempt more difficult versions.

The group may consist of any number of children, several playing the same kind of instrument; or it may just be a duet—piano and another instrument. Folk songs, marches, popular songs—almost anything may be used. No particular rhythm or pattern is necessary, but it is important that the children play on the beat or halfway between the beats and not at haphazard intervals. With many repetitions and refinements of the same piece, a fine sense of rhythm may thus be developed in the child under the guidance of a resourceful parent. If the parent does not play the piano, the phonograph can substitute. *Marche Militaire* or *Moments Musicaux* by Schubert, the marches by Sousa, the *Three English Dances* by German are good beginning numbers.

The only danger is that the rhythm band will become so expert that it will not know when to disband. Such simple rhythmic exercise is likely to dwarf musical development if carried on past the kindergarten stage. Older children lacking in rhythmic sense will get it more successfully from association with more complete musical forms.

Eurhythmics

A more intensive program in the development of rhythm is provided by classes in eurhythmics. These classes combine a particular type of step or bodily movement with a particular unit in rhythm, usually according to a system devised by Dalcroze. They develop a keen sense of rhythm. Children enjoy them. However, it takes a specially trained teacher to use this system effectively.

Singing games

The many singing games, such as *Farmer in the Dell, London Bridge Is Falling Down, Musical Chairs,* etc., should not be forgotten. Here the piano is not essential. In some games the phonograph or even radio, may be used. Such games serve to merge music with other experiences. They furnish the type of association that gives music feeling and power.

Rhythmic feeling

Obviously, the feeling for rhythm is not located in one part of the body nor associated with any particular set of muscles. Once a child has learned a rhythm in one hand, he can execute it in the other hand or with either foot or any finger, within certain limits set by the child's muscular control. This does not presume any "transfer of training" but merely that the feeling for rhythm is a very centrally located function, which can be directed toward any muscle system in the body.

Ear playing

At this early stage, playing by ear is very valuable. It does not matter what the instrument is, nor the tune, nor how crude the results may be, any playing by ear is certain to be operating at the child's own level and taking him forward at his own speed. Nor should the parent feel that he is helpless in this matter. Many a parent who has never been able to play by ear has learned to do so with his child. It does not make any difference whether or not the parent can play by notes, he will find that a little fooling around at the piano, similar to what the child is doing, will give him a start in this pastime. Without any teacher, but with time and devotion, one can develop considerable ease and skill.

Radio and recordings

It is probably unnecessary to call attention to the value of radio and recordings in developing a love for music. A warning should be issued, however, not to select music which is too simple or restricted to one style. A child does not learn by going from the simple to the complex. He learns what is interesting, what has feeling for him. Just as he overcomes the difficulty of adult vocabulary when a subject interests him, so he makes the colorful crash chord his own, even though it be complex. Nothing will impoverish a child's musical appreciation more than restricting his diet to children's songs and folk tunes.

The role of the parent in this period of early development in musical feeling should now be obvious. It is doubtful, indeed, if the responsiblity for this training can be delegated to another. The parent knows the child and his intimate needs and desires in the world of tone. Regardless of any lack of musical ability or experience, he can probably do a better job than any professional teacher.

HOW CAN THE PARENT HELP

Sing to the child.

Play to the child.

Use activities with singing or playing. If the child is sitting in your lap, trot him in time with the accents of music. If you are carrying the child, sway your body with the music.

Play musical games: London Bridge, Musical Chairs. Make up others.

Match tones. Sing a tone and let the child match it; or have the child sing a tone and you match it.

Imitate animal sounds; the child will copy.

March to music—either piano or phonograph.

Have children skip to rhythm.

Sing altermate phrases of song with the child.

Make a water-glass xylophone by filling jelly glasses with different amounts of water to tune a scale. Let child do the filling.

Buy phonograph records—both children's and adults'.

Encourage ear playing.

Avoid intellectual analysis and explanation until the child is in his teens.

II

the purpose of music

Not moral

"TEACH YOUR BOY TO BLOW A HORN AND HE WILL never blow a safe." So read advertisements widely distributed over the country by concerns interested in selling musical instruments. Unfortunately the large brass bands organized in penal institutions contradict this assertion. Music lessions are no guarantee that the child will lead a moral life. Perhaps they help. We have no statistics to prove the case.

Not intellectual

Nor can we recommend music as a mind trainer. Frequently music study does involve some mental activity, but very little in music requires more than a minimum of such effort. Remarkable performances by inmates of psychopathic institutions refute all claims that musical performance requires outstanding rational powers.

Most parents are vague about their purposes when they provide music lessons for their child. And they are probably right in not attempting to analyze their purpose. The effect of music study is too complicated to be unraveled even by the trained psychologist. But let us touch on some of the usual objectives of parents and music teachers.

A vocation

Music as a vocation is usually foremost in the minds of the specialized teachers, though it is seldom more than a vague possibility to parents. Many teachers, however, go on the assumption that unless the child begins at a certain age and follows a certain precise course of study—the one the teacher presents—music as a vocation will forever be closed to him.

There is no truth in this. It is well known that a child who attempts to learn a foreign language after adolescence will probably master it less completely than one who begins at an earlier age. Yet he can achieve a considerable degree of success. He may offset certain pronunciation shortcomings by a larger vocabulary, and so on. Joseph Conrad who learned English in his maturity became one of England's master writers.

Similarly in music one may learn to play an instrument at any age. The belief in an age limitation is a superstition, but one so powerful, still, that most teachers are reluctant to take on older pupils.

The purpose of music

Regardless of what parents or teachers may plan, however, many students aspire to use their instruments to help pay their way through college or provide the cost of an auto or a vacation. And a surprising number succeed. I have known many students to earn as much as sixty dollars a week playing in dance or theatre orchestras while carrying on their school work.

There are hazards, however, in this method of working one's way through college. Late hours and questionable surroundings may put a strain on the student's physical and moral stamina. All too often the money comes too temptingly easy, and the student is lured away from his originally planned vocation into what appear to be brighter prospects. Too late, perhaps, he realizes that the musical vocation is unrewarding except for the very few—those blessed with more than musical capacity, those who are of certain personality types and who have business acumen and, perhaps, sheer good luck. The spotlight is fickle. The jazz player of twenty may already have reached his top. He may realize that and wish to turn to another profession. But he has acquired habits of easy spending which make it difficult for him to start at the bottom of the other profession.

Adult avocation

Again, looking into the long-range objectives, in choosing an instrument the parent should consider what use will be made of it in adult life.

On Brass instruments: for example, daily practice is required to keep in form, to an extent that few adults find possible. Even the wood winds are difficult to play for more than a few minutes, if the player has not been practicing consistently.

String players and pianists also feel the lack of practice, but are able to play their instruments with some degree of satisfaction even after months without practice. Consequently, adults who play the wind instruments for fun are few. String players and pianists, on the other hand, frequently form groups to play quartets, trios, and duos. Some meet weekly year after year and find, if we may judge by their enthusiasm and devotion, one of the most cultural and enjoyable avocations available today. This is discussed in greater detail in the chapters on the separate instruments. (VI to XII).

Recreation

When I was a boy, there were these things to anticipate—a dance or a play scheduled many weeks ahead and choir rehearsal once a week. Other than that we had to plan our own entertainment. No movies then, no radio, no television, no extra-curricular activities at school, no gossiping, even, over the phone. There was plenty of time to fill. And music filled it delightfully.

Despite today's many new resources, parents wisely continue to provide music for their children, indeed more now than before, as a good means to fill out the after-school hours. But the new conditions have made the task of music teachers harder than ever before. The new resources and the new activities available to children are very enticing. A child cannot take on the daily schedule of an adult. If left with too little free time he will take his freedom in the scheduled time. Since music practice has the laxest supervision it is generally the first to suffer.

We all vary in our ability to stick to a tight schedule. We vary not only from person to person but also from day to day. Thus spring fever is mainly a revolt against the restraint and regularity of winter duties. Both the school year and the music year start off with fervor and high ambition. But there is football and the autumn holidays, then basketball and the Christmas rush, school plays, church affairs. Again and again practice is skimped or postponed. Music faces stiff competition indeed. The wise parents will watch the child's fluctuations with an understanding eye and will make adjustments accordingly.

Social

What chiefly draws the child to music is the social factor. He may crave the prestige some playmate has gained through public performance; he may see himself as the "life of the party" when he has mastered his instrument. In his later teens, he may turn to music as a means of gaining new acquaintances. School bands, orchestras, and glee clubs frequently supply the incentive. Thus in most cases the child has some social motive in seeking music lessons.

Physical pleasure

Although few people realize it, there is no small amount of direct physical pleasure in singing or in playing an instrument. Skill appeals to the child. He admires it in others, he craves it for himself. Adults are often annoyed by a child clapping his hands, tapping the table, swinging his feet, or clicking his tongue. The child enjoys such movements not merely for the noise but because the rhythmic, muscular motion is satisfying. There is a certain skill in doing it just right. The less active adult would be bored with the repetition of such strenuous muscular activity; however, let him remember how he lets his eye muscles follow the running design entirely around the church during a dull sermon. The child gets the same satisfaction from his more energetic muscular activity. Such rhythmical use of the muscles is often as complicated as the most intricate dances. Music serves to accentuate the physical thrill. This enjoyment is more vivid in the advanced stages of performance. Even the beginner, however, is often held longer at his practice by the fun of manipulating his own muscles.

Self-discipline

Music may also help in developing self-discipline, since the pupil is left to his own resources for longer periods than in his other studies. "I only made three mistakes that time." "I only made one mistake that time." "I played it without any mistake." "I played it three times without any mistake." Thus the child seeks sympathetic approbation from the parent. How strikingly similar to the exclamations the adult makes after a game of golf! Self-competition is the strongest motive in self-discipline for the child.

But music lessons may become a disintegrating force, if the lessons and practice are irregular and the child cannot bring himself to organize his practice. A good teacher encourages organization of the material and self-discipline follows.

Culture

One father told me he felt the music lessons were worth while, if for nothing else, because the child used the piano to let off steam. His son might come home feeling out of sorts. He would go to the piano and bang out some chords. Gradually he would fall into the mood of the music before him. In half an hour he would come away from the piano relieved and amiable. Such is the refining influence of culture.

Refinement or culture is probably the most widely held objective for the study of music. Culture is hard to define, but most people who are interested in music lessons for their children have a vague but insistent feeling that music has high cultural value and its possession will enrich their children's lives.

III

playing by ear

A CHILD LEARNS TO TALK BY FIRST MAKING queer squealings, high and low, loud and soft. These, with numberless repetitions and refinements, gain perfection by imitation and gain significance as they bring the results desired by the child. The child does not *consciously* manipulate his vocal cords to attain his results; he *thinks* his tone, and the muscles respond with increasing accuracy as he repeats his exercises.

His behavior is similar when learning music, which is another sort of language. If the child is to attain a mastery of the complex mechanism of the piano approaching the control he has over his vocal cords, we should expect him to begin with queer poundings on the piano, gradually refining these into higher and lower chords and discords, melodies and longer tunes. An approximation of this procedure on the violin, a much more intimate and therefore more contagious instrument than the piano, has resulted in some phenomenal child prodigies. This is a wonderful preparation for the appreciation of music.

Piano prodigies, however, usually do not develop by such a procedure. It may be that they *do* enjoy their music. But with the usual teaching methods it is more likely that when the tot climbs on the piano stool and gives an accurate rendering of a simple piece of Mozart, he has no more appreciation of that music than has the player roll. The many repetitions, the restrictions, the catchwords, pictures, colors and other non-musical devices which have been used to insure such precision are not conducive to enjoyment. Rather they tend to develop a forbidding conception of music which makes appreciation forever improbable. Much better the crude but satisfying thumping on the piano, that expresses or fulfills some actual desire within the child. This can be refined sooner or later into appreciation of the beautiful in sound.

As soon as a child thumps notes at the top of the keyboard and then at the bottom with the intention of hearing high notes and low notes, *he is playing by ear.* He is getting acquainted with the piano, and the ear is his guide. The same process can be observed when an older child takes up an unfamiliar instrument and begins to investigate how it works. He fools around with it until his ear has told him what sounds will come forth from the various keys and holes. Immediately he begins to put the tones in order; that is, he begins to play a piece. Then he tries another piece, and another. There is no limit to how far he may go. He may play things he has heard before, or he may originate new combinations and repeat them because he enjoys them, until he has a composition.

In reading music the player looks at the note on the page and then puts down a certain finger on a certain key or string or valve. It is presumed that he will listen to the sound that is produced; but there is no guarantee that he will. In playing by ear, on the other hand, the player listens to the note in his inner ear, or auditory memory, and then puts down his finger on a certain key or string or valve. He *must* listen to the note, for his ear is his only means of checking it. There can be no doubt which is the more musical process.

What limits playing by ear is that the advanced player, when he attempts it, finds himself suddenly restricted to elementary pieces. But the player who has learned by ear finds himself in the same predicament when he tries to read music. He, too, is then suddenly restricted to elementary pieces. Each, of course, has concentrated on one process to the neglect of the other. It would have been better had the two processes developed simultaneously.

Children prefer to play by ear, since it avoids the monotony of learning notes. But ear playing will not develop as fast as note reading, if the teacher gives all attention to the latter and leaves ear playing to develop on its own. With just a little encouragement ear playing develops rapidly. The parent can help here by suggesting suitable tunes.

Frequently the child plays popular music by ear. He hears the jazz tune or the swooning melody over the radio and tries to reproduce it. The teacher does not give him this type of piece, and he cannot find the music for it. He learns it the only way he can—by ear.

There is no reason why he should not do so. Popular music is not bad. It is merely a few simple chords and rhythms strung together with a few harmonic novelties or effects currently in style. Shorn of these novelties they resemble folk music. That is why they are popular. Indeed, our greatly honored body of folk music and "melody favorites" originated in just this way.

Since both folk music and popular music are constructed from simple harmonies, they are particularly well suited to ear playing. Where these tunes are incompletely learned by ear, it is well to provide the child with sheet music, from which the exact chord or melodic phrase that has been sought unsuccessfully can be mastered. The child will probably not continue to use the music, but he has added a few more chords to his playing vocabulary.

Ear playing involves two distinct activities: first, the player must *remember* what he has heard; second, he must be able to find with his fingers the tones he hears in his ear, or, more scientifically, in his auditory memory. In talking and singing, this second process entails no difficulty at all, since the vocal cords are so perfectly under control that they shape the proper sound as soon as it is thought. But when an instrument is used, becoming completely intimate with the keys and finger holes is no simple matter. It is easier to find the right key when the memory of the music is very vivid.

For some reason or other, however, a few children never attempt to play by ear, or, if they do, are discouraged before they have enough success to enjoy it. For these the parent can do much. Suggest tunes with a limited range and let the child develop by gradually undertaking more complicated melodies. If the piano is his instrument, these tunes can be played in the key of C and harmonized by the following three chords, which may be selected at random by ear: C-E-G, C-F-A, B-D-G. The easiest key for playing by ear varies with different instruments, but it is well for the ear player not to confine his efforts to one key. The following pieces are arranged in order of difficulty, and the first note is indicated for playing in the key of C.

Mary Had a Little Lamb	E
Three Blind Mice	E
America	C
Yankee Doodle	C
Dixie	G

THE FARMER'S IN THE DELL	G
SWANEE RIVER	E
MY OLD KENTUCKY HOME	E
O, SUSANNA	C
SILENT NIGHT	G
THE BRAHMS LULLABY	E
THE STAR-SPANGLED BANNER	G

After playing these in the key of C, the child should experiment until he can play them in other keys.

Any piece which does not modulate, that is, does not have sharps and flats scattered throughout the piece, will be easy to play. Once the child has figured out a few of these on the list, he will discover others of his own accord. Nor do children take them in order of difficulty. Often something in the more difficult piece catches the ear, making it easier to work out than the simple piece. Of course, ear playing is almost impossible unless the child *wants* to play the number. His own impulses are usually best.

There will be many mistakes when music is learned by ear. The results will be no more accurate than the player's ear. But this is precisely the advantage of ear playing over note playing; the latter develops a mental and physical activity without any assurance that the ear is even active. These mistakes are not dangerous habits. They are similar to inaccuracies in pronunciation when learning a new language. When the ear has improved, they will disappear.

The final proof, however, that ear playing is good for the child, is that he enjoys it. Any procedure which helps the child to *enjoy* the music is naturally good.

HOW CAN THE PARENT HELP

Suggest tunes to play by ear.

When the child makes up tunes, write them down, if you can.

Help the child to find the first note of the piece.

Let the child try different instruments.

On the piano, encourage the child to "chord" tunes, when he has captured the melody.

Help the child to find these chords—the harmony. The following table gives the three most used chords in each of the six favorite keys for ear playing on the piano.

Keynote	*Tonic*	*Subdominant*	*Dominant*
C	C-E-G	C-F-A	B-D-G
G	G-B-D	G-C-E	F♯-A-D
F	F-A-C	F-B♭-D	E-G-C
B♭	B♭-D-F	B♭-E♭-G	A-C-F
E♭	E♭-G-B♭	E♭-A♭-C	D-F-B♭
D	D-F♯-A	D-G-B	C♯-E-A

Ask for further advice from someone who plays by ear.

Learn yourself to play by ear.

IV

practice

THERE IS NO GREATER PROBLEM IN THE TEACHING of music than practice. It is here that the teaching most often fails, turning from a music problem into a behavior problem. It is here that the parent, in his very eagerness to forward the child's musical development, does most to hinder it and often sets up conflicts that prevent musical growth.

The ideal practice is that which is done voluntarily. And practice is voluntary only to the degree that the child gets satisfaction from it. This depends upon many intangible things. There is the sheer physical fun it often affords. For just as it is fun to attempt to juggle three balls at a time, so it is fun to jump from chord to chord. It is fun to play a scale in fast tempo and astonish even oneself by the speed. There is fun in putting the material in order, even the simple material of the early lessons; it is like putting a puzzle together.

There is also fun in getting the job done, even though it may not be enjoyable at the moment. The alarm clock that the child sets on top of the piano to indicate the exact moment at which the practice hour ends is an indication of the determination to at least finish the task. Some children *enjoy* their ambitions to excel on the musical instrument, to display greater skill than any of their playmates. While practicing they may daydream about their goal of achievement. But such daydreaming has its value and is not injurious to the practice.

The chief joy in practice, however, comes from the opportunity for self-expression. The restrictions and etiquette of society drastically confine the normal exuberant child. Music can provide outlets for his feelings, whether they be enthusiasm or disgust, love or hate. This is hardly possible in the beginning, but it is surprising how much feeling a youngster can pack into a little melody, entirely unobserved by the casual listener. Here begins the satisfaction in music which makes it eventually a powerful art for the child. But all such satisfactions depend upon the child's being alone. Fantasies will burst like soap bubbles when the parent interrupts with a criticism or a suggestion.

Alone

It is very difficult, however, for the parent to stay out of the scene. On hearing a wrong note repeated he feels that it simply must be corrected. Yet if he corrects one misplayed note he feels that he must correct others; he begins to assume the teacher's responsibility. But the child rightly considers himself responsible to the *teacher* for his wrong notes and feels victimized by the parent's interference.

Alone

Fooling around with the instrument, the making of noise just for the sake of noise, even the playing of intentional wrong notes must be overlooked. This resembles the learning of the correct pronunciation of a word by successive, trial mispronunciations. It seems mere horseplay at the time but it has a useful function. Similar horseplay with musical notes should be tolerated for the same reason. The child is not yet advanced enough to get fun, musically, by correct sequences. Therefore he takes his fun as he can in the crude sounds he is able to make. From this he will work his way to more musical sound. The important thing is that he should enjoy the process.

Alone

Probably nothing discounts a child's practice more than having a playmate sitting by, waiting for him to finish the practice. Even the knowledge that someone is waiting in another room or on the doorstep will undermine the precarious concentration and make the practice worthless. Better then to skip the practice period.

Length

The length of time for practice should be individually adjusted to each child. Any child can practice effectively by himself for fifteen minutes. A child of eight or nine can practice effectively for at least half an hour. By the time he is twelve and in the seventh grade at school, one hour is not too much at a time, *if* done when he is not tired, mentally or physically. By high-school age, with its intemperate expenditures of energy and bursts of enthusiasm, it may be difficult to restrain a youngster under two, three, or even four hours of practice. This is probably the only period when a child is likely to practice too much. His health and exuberance must be the indication of where the limit shall be drawn.

Various instruments

The desirable length of practice period also varies with the instrument. Wind instruments, particularly during the first six months, cannot have the long, uninterrupted practice periods possible on the piano. And the same is true of voice. In such cases it is desirable to break the practice period up into ten-minute periods and then gradually to increase them as the muscles involved become accustomed to the new usage. With the string instruments the difficulty is not with the muscles used in playing the instrument but rather those involved in maintaining the playing posture. Similarly, it is not the finger muscles which tire in piano practice, but rather the muscles of the back. Violinists frequently walk around as they practice, and the pianist would do well to stretch occasionally. Children will naturally relieve themselves by such changes of posture unless they are kept rigid, during practice, by a feeling of restraint or compulsion.

Parents generally feel bound, however, by the time they consider proper, rather than setting it as

The lower limit

an upper limit. A child's practice time is definitely an individual problem. To develop into a virtuoso, a child must always be kept practicing up to the very limit. If the child is being taught merely to "be able to play a bit for fun" he need practice only intermittently. Any adequate teacher can give him that much during his lesson periods. The normal objective lies between these two extremes. The parent should let the teacher know what he wishes. In any case, the objective should be left open to modification after the pupil's reaction becomes apparent. This may seem an indifferent policy. The amount of *effective* practice that is possible is, however, so dependent upon the child's attitude, that no safe general rule can be given.

Most teachers request an hour of daily practice. Serious advanced students, of course, practice more. The average pupil does under an hour a day, even with Sundays, Saturdays, and lesson days omitted. The long practice periods of a generation ago are seldom found today. With so much musical experience coming from radio and recordings, they are probably not necessary. Certainly in the crowded programs of modern children, they are not easy to realize. Moreover, it may be that shorter practice is counteracted by today's better teaching methods.

A pupil in his teens may be made to realize that the cost of his lessons is inversely proportionate to his amount of practice. Two hundred hours of practice scattered out over two years will be just twice as expensive as two hundred hours of practice in one year, since twice as many lessons must be paid for. And it is likely that the two hundred hours of practice concentrated in one year will produce better results than a desultory two hundred hours spread out over a longer period.

Regular time

Practicing has this resemblance to swimming—the hardest step is the first, the jumping into it. The plunge into something so confining as musical practice is resisted, but once in, the practice often becomes fun and is continued beyond the clock limit that has been set.

By gentle reminder, or insistence if necessary, the parent can do much to make the plunge easier. The easiest way to accomplish this is by setting a regular daily time for practice. It then becomes as much a matter of course as going to school at the same hour each day. Morning is generally the most effective time. Some children, however, do splendid work in the evening, when they are relaxed and have a feeling of leisure. Since this is generally a time for recreation, an evening hour may prove unwise, especially if the practice comes in competition with radio and television.

Avoid competition

This points to the chief contribution that the parent can make to encourage practice—removal of competing temptations. If playmates or other members of the family go off to a movie, while the child is kept at home practicing, he will come to resent the music which keeps him shut in. The parent must avoid this type of conflict.

Repetition

Although what goes on during the practice period should be a problem between teacher and pupil, the parent may help by sympathetic understanding. Most teachers require considerable repetition of small sections of the music. The child dislikes the repetition and tends to play on to the end and then go to the next piece. It is difficult, even for the teacher, to determine how much repetition to insist on. When much repetition does take place, the parent might help by commenting favorably on it after the practice is over. The amount of attention paid to fingering, to phrasing, to expression, to accuracy, to technique must be determined by the teacher. A good teacher will adjust procedure or emphasis to the individual student.

Memorization

Whether or not the music is memorized is again something to be determined by the teacher. It depends upon how easily memorizing is done and upon the particular piece being studied. The maturity of the child often influences the decision.

The parent, then, should provide a convenient situation for practice and then adopt a policy of "hands off." The interest of the parent in the music produced, best indicated by his enthusiasm for pieces the child plays, will largely determine the importance which the child places upon his music study. If the child feels that his music is important enough, he will take care of the practice in his own way; and that practice will not only be the best type of practice for his music but will also be a strong factor in developing self-discipline.

HOW CAN THE PARENT HELP

Remove counter attractions.

Set a time for the practice and arrange to be at home, if possible, so he has company (not for policing him!). *Early morning* is best; many find *evening* a good time; *noon* is all right; *after school,* before playing, may work, but the child is tired of restraint and tends to get it over with in a hurry; *after play* seldom works.

Encourage practice on Saturday and Sunday; it tends to make practice classify as fun rather than as work.

Do not expect the child to practice after his lesson; tension has been released and he should not be called upon to undergo a further strain.

Bargain for favors; you will do this, if he gets his practicing done. Or, better still, you will do this job of his, so that he can get his practicing done. But be careful to present it as cooperation; do not allow him to feel that practice is a penalty or unpleasant job to be done.

Smaller children like to have gold stars to paste on the wall or a card to be punched, when the practice is completed satisfactorily.

Rewards help sometimes.

Keep an optimistic and not a defeatist attitude before the child. "He likes it!" "He is doing better now!" "It is easy for him!" The child's total reaction is sometimes set by suggestion.

Let the child know that you enjoy his practice —you do not just tolerate it. Admit that you couldn't do it yourself. Tell others how you enjoy it. Let him feel that it is very much worth while—not in the dim and distant future—but right now.

V

musical talent

Talent not important

ANY NORMAL CHILD CAN LEARN TO PLAY AN INstrument. Every normal child learns to talk though the mechanism of the voice requires more sensitive control than the most complicated musical instrument. Some children do not learn to talk as early as others; some never can be great orators or distinguished actors. These differences or limitations might be explained as talent or a lack of talent in the art of speech. But no one would question a child's ability to learn to talk effectively despite lack of such talent. The case is no different with music. Some children will take to music at a much earlier age than others; some never can become great singers or virtuosi; but any normal child can learn to play. The question of talent need not be considered until the child has become more than a satisfactory performer on his chosen musical instrument.

Variations in talent

If we disregard talent how do we then account for the great differences in children's success with music, even at an early age? In the same way that we account for children's differences in their command of language at an early age. A child who comes from an illiterate home will have a smaller vocabulary and make more grammatical errors than the child from the cultured home.

Similarly, a child from a musically illiterate home will have a more limited response to music than the child from a musical home. General Grant is reported to have said that he could recognize only two tunes: *Yankee Doodle,* and every other tune. In a time when music was heard as seldom as a foreign language, such a case might well be true. But with the omnipresence of radio and its wealth of music of all kinds, such musical illiteracy is no longer possible. Musical literacy can be easily attained by careful choice of records, by attending concerts, and by selecting the more interesting programs available on the radio.

Absolute pitch

One ability which a few children have requires special mention. That is *absolute pitch,* sometimes mistakenly called *perfect pitch.* Musicians are not agreed on just what the term means, but it is generally conceded that a person has absolute pitch if he can name a tone when he hears it or can sing a particular tone without hearing it first. What it amounts to is an accurate memory of pitch. It is comparable to the ability of some people to carry an exact color in their mind and match it exactly at some later time. We have had no success in teaching absolute pitch in America, and no one knows just why some children acquire the ability and others do not.

On the European continent this ability is taught as a matter of course. Their success is probably due to their use of stationary syllables. On the continent *do* always refers to C, *re* to D, *mi* to E, etc. In England and America, on the contrary, *do* refers to the first tone of the scale. If the piece is in the key of C *do* is C; if the piece is in the key of D, *do* is D; if the piece is in the key of E, *do* is E, etc. And all of the other syllables, of course, fluctuate accordingly. The continental system focuses the attention upon absolute pitch. Our system of movable syllables focuses the attention upon relative pitch.

In America absolute pitch is thus left to chance development. Some people have it in a limited degree; they can name a pitch when they hear it on the violin but not on the piano, etc. It is a will-o'-the-wisp with many people, but there are those who are as certain of the name of the pitch they hear as they are of the name of the key they see on the piano. Many of the great composers and conductors have absolute pitch; many do not. It is not essential to success in music but it is a great advantage.

In selecting a particular instrument, physical limitations which may prove a handicap on certain in-

Talent for a particular instrument

struments should be taken into account. The hand which cannot stretch an octave at the piano is at a decided disadvantage though there have been pianists with small hands who have put forth the extra effort necessary to achieve the concert stage. Malformation of the teeth sometimes makes a brass instrument impractical. And it takes a sturdy youngster to carry a huge bass horn on parade. A short-legged person is at a disadvantage on the organ. Though such physical limitations are handicaps, they may be overcome. All too often hidden physical handicaps are alleged by an inadequate teacher to explain a pupil's lack of satisfactory progress. Very little is known about musical talent and psychologists have thus far been unable to devise tests which will predict success in music with accuracy at all comparable to the tests sometimes used to predict success in school subjects.

Tests for talent

Nevertheless, many a respectable music educator and psychologist today, in all good faith, gives tests which presume to determine the amount of musical talent a child has.

Yet it should be obvious to anyone that a test which declares a child untalented because he fails to recognize a variation in pitch of two or three vibrations, must be false. The violinist, who probably depends more than any other musician upon fine differences in pitch, constantly uses a vibrato, sometimes called *tremolo,* which varies in pitch many times more than this. And other tests which measure sensitivity to time, to rhythm, to loudness, etc., are no more useful. No matter how accurate, the measurement has nothing to do with a child's success in music. On a similar assumption one might attempt to estimate a child's capacity to become a painter by measuring how far he can see. Success in music is dependent upon too many factors and is too complicated a mechanism to be forecast by any methods known today.

False tests

However, like patent medicines, new tests are constantly being advertised. Parents eager to discover talent in their children are preyed upon by instrument manufacturers who beguile them into buying instruments for children who may never use them effectively, if at all. In one large city I encountered a "psychologist" who was doing a rushing business administering such "tests" at ten dollars apiece. I am constantly beset by parents who want me to give such tests to their offspring. To my explanations of their futility the parents usually reply they "would like to have the child take the test anyhow." On one occasion the parent sat by the child and whispered the right answer every time the child made a mistake!

Parent responsibility

The parent's responsibility in the child's musical development is something more complex than the discovery of talent. It involves showing a sustained interest in the child's experiences with music, a patient listening to his first attempts, an understanding of his relations with playmates who may or may not be taking music lessons, a searching out of musical groups with whom he can participate. The important thing is to make it possible in every way for the child to like music; given the proper conditions he will.

HOW CAN THE PARENT HELP

Have confidence in the child.

Never say, "He has no talent." Instead, state the positive factors, however small. "He likes to play rather than sing." "He spends a lot of time just amusing himself at the instrument." You do not know how much talent there may be there!

VI

the choice of an instrument

Available literature

INSTRUMENTS VARY GREATLY IN THEIR CAPACITY to provide musical training or culture. The literature or repertory available for some instruments is too limited. Other instruments are effective or useful only in orchestras or bands. The great composers have written for only a few of the many instruments in use today. Present-day composers are writing for some of the neglected instruments, but the number of instruments with an adequate literature remains small. In general, these are the instruments which one hears in concert solo performances. If a child selects an instrument without a literature, that instrument must always remain an expensive plaything. Oftentimes the chief reason a child wishes to play an instrument is to join an orchestra or band.

Use in groups

Is the instrument the child wants to learn used in the school orchestra? Is it used in the band? Can it be used in small groups of players? The children know the answers to most of these questions. Indeed, often the orchestra or band director at school, in need of a particular instrument, makes it a point to interest certain children in it. This may be a good instrument for the child, but the parent should guard against such a choice unless there are other reasons for undertaking it. Instruments vary greatly in popularity from time to time and place to place. The choice may go to the instrument that the conductor uses or the parent plays, the instrument featured in a certain movie, radio program, or television show, or that is displayed, with pearl inlay and brightly polished in the local music-store window.

Demand

If the child is interested in an instrument chiefly for its social value, the opportunities for the instrument should be a consideration. Some instruments, like the oboe, French horn, and the cello, are always in demand in orchestras. The child who plays one of these instruments will be much sought after. Other instruments, such as saxophone and cornet, are favorites of children and are therefore more than plentiful. A youngster playing such an instrument may not be able to get into an organization unless he is very good.

Prestige

Closely connected with the demand for the instrument is its prestige. Parents seldom realize the aristocratic position which some instruments occupy in the hierarchy of adolescent estimation. This varies greatly in different localities and at different ages. In general there is more prestige attached to the loud instruments than to the soft, to the shiny instruments than to the dull black ones, to the large instruments than to the small ones. But rarity is the chief factor. Prestige, however, cannot be long maintained without practice; this is frequently the most powerful motive in keeping a child at his practice.

Practice

More practice is required on some instruments than on others to acquire sufficient mastery to appear in any capacity in public. Any instrument requires a lifetime of devotion to rise to the top, because there are always those who are willing to devote a lifetime to gain supremacy. But it is the length of the preparatory period of practice a child must undergo before he can show off his ability to others that makes one instrument more precarious an undertaking than another. Some youngsters are unwilling to practice two years before they are "good enough to get in the orchestra." Such children must select an instrument which brings quick results, like the recorder, even though it may not hold his interest later on. In such a case there may be a shift to a related instrument of greater value. Similarly, the child may shift from bugle to trumpet, or from mellophone to French horn, or from saxophone to oboe or bassoon. For the piano and string instruments, however, there is no steppingstone. The appeal must be a direct one and strong enough to carry through the initial period of practice necessary before public appearance is feasible.

DATA ABOUT INSTRUMENTS

	Literature available	Difficulty of keeping in practice	Used in			Transposing	Demand	Prestige	Cost	Upkeep per year	Difficulty of carrying	Average Age of beginner
			Orchestra	Band	Ensemble				$	$		
Piano	fine	easy	..	..	X	no	great	much	50-1500	12	none	8
Organ	fine	very easy	..	..	..	no	small	much	900 up	10	none	12
Harp	good	medium	X	..	X	no	great	much	600-2000	25	great	12
Violin	fine	difficult	X	..	X	no	great	much	25-150	10	some	7
Viola	good	medium	X	..	X	no*	great	average	40-150	10	some	12
Cello	fine	difficult	X	..	X	no*	great	much	60-200	15	great	8
String Bass	none	easy	X	X	X	no	average	average	80-300	15	great	16
Flute	good	medium	X	X	X	no	average	average	100-300	10	little	12
Oboe	poor	difficult	X	X	X	no	great	average	100-350	20	little	12
Clarinet	good	difficult	X	X	X	yes	average	average	40-180	20	little	10
Saxophone	poor	easy	..	X	..	yes	small	little	60-300	20	some	10
Bassoon	poor	medium	X	X	X	no*	average	little	100-700	20	some	14
French Horn	poor	very difficult	X	X	X	yes	great	much	100-300	0	some	12
Trumpet	poor	very difficult	X	X	..	yes	small	aver-	50-200	0	little	12
Cornet	poor	very difficult	..	X	..	yes	small	little	40-150	0	little	12
Trombone	poor	very difficult	X	X	..	no*	average	average	60-250	0	some	14
Tuba	none	easy	X	X	..	no	small	little	100-350	0	great	16

*While these instruments are of the non-transposing variety, the student must learn the alto clef in the case of the Viola, and the tenor clef in addition to the bass clef in the case of the Cello, Bassoon and Trombone.

Difficulty of keeping in practice

Another factor to be considered in choosing an instrument is the ease or difficulty of keeping in practice. Few children or adults are devoted enough to music to be successful on an instrument which requires continuous daily practice. A good organist can sit down after a year's absence from the organ bench and few people will be aware that he has not been practicing the past week. Wood-wind and brass players are not so fortunate. Without constant practice the muscles, used in playing the instrument, grow too flabby for proper performance and many players finally give up.

Cost

The cost of the instrument is another consideration. It is probably best not to invest too heavily in the first instrument or even to start the child on a rented instrument. While it is true that an expensive instrument is always easier to play than a cheap one, and that good tone is sometimes impossible on a poor instrument, it must be remembered that a beginner does not know what kind of an instrument he will eventually want. He is happy with even the cheapest of instruments. Moreover, there is no greater stimulus to practice than acquiring a better instrument. The parent might do well to wait until the initial spurt of enthusiasm has burned itself out and then trade the first purchase for a new instrument. By this time the child has very definite ideas about what he wants and will be able to appreciate a fine instrument.

Upkeep

In this connection the upkeep of an instrument

should be considered. The bows of the string instruments must be rehaired occasionally and the strings break frequently. Harps mean a big bill for transportation. The wood-wind instruments have to be repadded and the reed instruments require a continuous supply of new reeds. These are just the normal monthly expenditures to keep an instrument in good playing condition. There are still the repairs necessary in case the instrument is dropped or otherwise abused. Even the piano requires the tuner.

Thus no simple formula can be given for the choice of an instrument. In addition to the considerations already noted there are others such as the difficulty of carrying the instrument to and from school, the age at which a child may successfully undertake an instrument, the need of a place to practice without provoking complaints from neighbors.

Transposing instruments

Some children and parents are disappointed when they discover that the new instrument cannot play from the same music as the piano. This happens when the instrument is a *transposing instrument.* When the child is playing the piano, or any other non-transposing instrument, he produces the sound of C when he plays C. When he is playing a transposing instrument he does not produce the sound C when he reads and plays C, but another, depending on the special key to which the transposing instrument is pitched. These will be discussed separately in the chapters on the separate instruments. To the layman this seems ridiculous, and there actually is not much justification for such a practice today. But we cannot reform the entire music profession overnight, so we must accept the situation. It is possible for the player to learn to read the notation from the piano copy by using a different fingering on his instrument, and all good professional players do this. Nor does it present any great difficulty to the beginner, if he is willing to learn two sets of fingering for his instrument. Nevertheless, very few children do learn this transposition.

All these factors are charted on the opening page of this chapter so that the parent may have before him all the considerations he should have in mind in choosing an instrument. In the following four chapters they are further discussed for particular instruments.

HOW CAN THE PARENT HELP

Let the child hear the instrument desired in advantageous circumstances.

Get pictures of the instrument.

Look at the instruments in the windows and showcases of the music stores.

Find other children or adults who are enthusiastic about an instrument.

Buy recordings of solos by the instrument.

Tell anecdotes about the instruments.

VII

the piano, organ, and harp

Popularity

THE PIANO HAS BEEN THE MOST POPULAR INstrument for over a century. A glance at the directory of music teachers in town will show more teachers of piano than of all other instruments combined. One reason for this is that so much music can be played on the piano, more having been composed for the piano than for any other instrument. Singers and instrument soloists require a pianist for their accompaniment. All the popular music is available for the piano. Indeed there is scarcely a composition in the entire realm of music that is not available in some edition for piano.

Insensitivity to pitch

But there are also offsetting disadvantages. Because the child does not have to control the pitch on the piano, he is likely to become indifferent to it, or just punch the right key and let the pitch take care of itself. The result may be a player who has little ear for music. The enjoyment of music depends upon hearing it sensitively; and accurate performance does not necessarily guarantee this type of listening. Most children do listen critically to the tones they are producing on the piano; the others soon tire of their lessons. The best insurance that a child will listen to what he is doing is to encourage him to play by ear, until he wants to read notes and then he will do both.

Notation

Teachers of other instruments prefer that the child should first have studied piano because he then knows his notation. The keyboard instruments are the only ones which use two clefs simultaneously—the bass, 𝄢, and the treble clef, 𝄞. The beginning pianist learns these just as he learns the alphabet in reading English. Since practically all of the other instruments use one of these two clefs, a beginner on another instrument who has had a year or two of piano, is at a decided advantage.

Not in orchestra

The chief disadvantage of the piano from the child's point of view is that it is not used in the orchestra. Dance bands include a pianist, but not the big school orchestras. However, the small school orchestras frequently use a pianist or two for general background or to fill in the missing parts. This is fine musical experience for the pianist and very enjoyable, but he seldom has a real piano part to play. Often the pianist plays drums or cymbals in the orchestra, or takes up some other instrument which the school orchestra is lacking and which the pianist can pick up very quickly.

Ensembles

The lack of a regular place in the orchestra is compensated for by the many ensemble opportunities for even the young pianist. There is an enormous quantity of literature for the trio—piano, violin, and cello. This ranges from masterworks by the great composers down to arrangements of folk songs and popular tunes, which can be played by beginners. The same is true of duos for violin and piano, cello and piano, flute and piano, clarinet and piano, etc. And for the advanced player there are the famous piano quartets, for piano, violin, viola, and cello, and the piano quintets for piano and string quartet. Indeed, most of the literature for other instruments includes a piano. These combinations often function in adult life and are social assets of the first order. They should be encouraged at all ages.

THE PIANO

Social advantage

Because of these many demands upon the piano, it is the instrument of greatest social appeal. At parties the piano is needed whether there be singing or instrumental playing. Although only one pianist is used at a time, the pianists usually take turns and everyone is happy. Here the ability to play by ear is particularly important. The person who can provide each new tune as it is called for becomes the life of the party.

Keeping in practice on the piano is not as difficult as on most instruments. Although performances at

Keeping in practice

anything approaching virtuosity standards requires almost daily devotion, the average pianist can play passably though he has not practiced for months. This makes the piano the most practical instrument for the adult. Once he has learned to play for fun, he seldom loses the knack.

Literature

Since keyboard instruments have been popular for over three hundred years now, the literature for them is enormous. There is plenty of music for all ages, at all stages of difficulty, and for all occasions. There is no danger that the student having learnt the instrument will find everything written for it too childish to hold his interest. The greatest masters have written some of their finest work for this medium; and the most humble folk song is effective on the piano. This extensive literature is the greatest recommendation for studying the piano.

Cost and quality

The cost of a piano has great latitude, since it figures in the household not only as a musical instrument but also as a piece of display furniture. Any secondhand instrument which will stay in tune will do for the beginner; but it is hard to tell whether it will. The pegs to which the strings are fastened may slip out of place almost as fast as the tuner puts them in. If the piano is much below pitch, it is doubtful if it can be maintained in pitch. It is easier for the tuner to tune the piano down than to tune it up. Consequently, irresponsible tuners gradually lower the pitch of the instrument. After this has been done over a period of years, the piano will not stay up on pitch, even though a good tuner does pull it up to concert pitch. However, if the old piano is still on pitch, it is the best guarantee that it will remain in tune. Secondhand pianos can be bought from the owners for as little as fifty dollars, if one is willing to wait and watch the classified ads in the newspaper. Dealers recondition these instruments and sell them at one hundred dollars up.

Size of piano

The most important factor in good piano tone is the length of the strings. Many devices have been used to compensate for short strings in the small models designed for apartments and small houses, but these devices are effective chiefly as texts for sales talk. The longer the strings the better the tone quality. This is why the long grand piano used in concert performance has such wonderful tone quality. Its length constitutes its chief advantage over models which use vertical strings. Similarly a full-size upright will have better tone than a tiny baby grand. A medium-sized baby grand piano is the finest for the home if space can be made for it. The term *baby grand* does not specify any particular size but popularly refers to any grand piano smaller than the big nine-foot concert instrument. Different manufacturers use the term to specify different models. The grand piano has other advantages over vertical models. Gravity pulls the hammers back into place in the grand pianos, whereas some arrangement of weighted leverage is required in the vertical models.

A dry room with even temperature is best for the

Place for piano

piano. The basement and the bedroom are the least desirable places to put a piano. A bedroom is bad because the sudden changes of temperature will crack the soundboard, if the window is opened at night. The cellar is likely to be even worse, for dampness is hard on a piano. Many parts are glued and may come apart; the ivories may come loose from the keys; and the veneer may peel off the case.

Humidity

On the other hand, the average living room is much too dry for the welfare of a piano during the winter, when artificial heat is on. Rattles develop and the soundboard is likely to crack. The best insurance against this is to increase the humidity in the room. This is as good for us as it is for the piano. A jar kept filled with water, with a sponge suspended inconspicuously in it to increase evaporation, may be placed under a grand piano. This need not be an eyesore and will safeguard the piano. A similar jar may be placed inside an upright piano, just a few inches above the floor, by removing the front panel above the pedals. Plants placed near the piano also help humidity—particularly if they are in water themselves.

If no better place can be found for the piano than the basement, then it is wise to buy a cheap instrument. Then if it is ruined the loss will not be great, and in any event the pleasure it will give will repay the investment. In some respects there are even advantages in not having the piano in the living room. A child tends to be self-conscious when he must practice in the presence of adults. It is healthy for him sometimes to wham away with abandon, just as it is healthy for him to shout, neither of which are permitted in the living room.

Tuning

Tuning is a problem. There are many theories about it, but the best rule seems to be to have the piano tuned twice a year—once after the furnace has been turned on in the fall and once when the furnace has been permanently turned off in the spring. It is the change of humidity rather than temperature which puts the piano out of tune. A concert pianist will soon knock a piano out of tune, but ordinary playing has no noticeable effect upon the tuning. Most people cannot tell when the piano needs tuning, unless it is very badly out of tune. The easiest way to determine this is to play octaves or single notes one after the other and to listen if they seem to buzz or vary in their tone quality. If the tone is clear and steady, the piano is not badly out of tune. On the other hand, a perfectly tuned piano tends to sound flat and less brilliant than before it was tuned. Owners often insist that the tuner has softened their instrument, and they do not like it. Consequently, some tuners intentionally leave the instrument slightly out of tune. The owner's best assurance of a good job is to use a tuner recommended by the piano teacher or someone who plays very well, and then rely on his judgment. The piano action is too complicated for any layman to understand; he must trust the advice of the expert tuner.

Age to begin

At just what age piano lessons should be begun is a question with many answers. Some teachers say, "The earlier the better," and take tots at the age of three, barely able to climb up on the piano bench. The teachers give them little tone games and simple scale sequences, which the children appear to enjoy. Progress is made at this age, but it is slow and therefore expensive, since the small child requires more frequent lessons than the child in his teens. There is also the danger that the child will take a dislike to the instrument before he is old enough to enjoy the fun of playing. Moreover, a child's eyes do not fixate easily and accurately enough at this age to make reading notation advisable. Big print is provided in many instruction books for the young child, but rote playing, not notation, should comprise most of the training at this time. At about eight, the child begins to read more easily and to learn more rapidly. This is the most profitable time to begin piano lessons.

The belief that older children or adults do not learn music as readily as small children is a myth. Some teachers may be more efficient at teaching one age than another, and there are some things which will be easier for children than for adults—but so are there many things that are easier for adults than for children. The chief difficulty is that the adult will be less satisfied with the first results and few adults will practice as regularly as children do. On reaching the age of fifteen or so the child is not willing to practice unless he is playing "grown-up" music. If by that time he cannot play music that interests his friends and adults, he will probably lose interest in his lessons. In this case, it is wise to change instruments.

An aid to other instruments

The piano is considered a valuable preliminary to the study of some other instrument or voice. The beginner does not play out of pitch, if the piano is in tune. He may play a wrong note; but if he strikes A, it will sound A—neither flat nor sharp. But if the fingers on the string instruments, or the lips on the wood-wind instruments, are not in exactly the right position, the note will be sour. Thus a child first trained on the piano knows the correct pitches, and when he changes to violin or trumpet the task of his teacher is made much easier.

THE ORGAN

There are three quite different instruments which today are called organs: (1) the reed organ, which used to grace every farmhouse parlor and is now being sought as a novelty instrument; (2) the pipe organ, found in all the bigger churches today; and (3) the electronic organ, which appeared just a couple of decades ago and is being used in funeral parlors and small churches. The electronic organ is frequently known as an *electric organ* but should not be confused with the pipe organ with electric action, which is sometimes also called an electric organ.

Few students study organ without first taking sev-

Piano first

eral years of piano lessons. The reed organ is more or less a plaything today and needs no special consideration. Any pianist can quickly learn to play a reed organ. His main difficulty is nothing more serious than keeping his feet pumping at the pedals without influencing his hands. He must also learn to connect the tones with the fingers, since the organ does not have the piano's sustaining pedal to accomplish the smooth connection. This is easily learned by any pianist sufficiently advanced to play hymns with ease.

The pipe-organ teacher, however, prefers that the student should have had enough piano study to be able to play Bach fugues. The chief difficulty in mastering the pipe-organ is learning to play on two different keyboards and a pedal board all at the same time without mixing the parts up. Bach fugues are a splendid training for this type of discipline. With this good background, progress on the organ is astonishingly rapid.

A special difficulty is to find an organ on which to practice. Most churches are not heated in the winter, and the organ student can therefore take lessons only in the warmer months. Churches usually charge from ten to seventy-five cents an hour for practice. However, the organ student may do at least half of his practicing on a piano; many organ teachers insist upon this, in order to keep the technique lively. For the speed and strength with which one strikes an organ key makes no difference in the tone; the mechanical stops or tablets must be manipulated to change the tone quality. This makes for a dead touch on the keys and the live touch of the piano is needed to counteract the effect.

Not too difficult

The organ is definitely a church instrument. Its cost and the amount of room necessary to house it make it impractical for all except the most luxurious homes. This is unfortunate, since it is probably the easiest of all instruments to play, if one has an adequate piano technique. Indeed, it seems much like conducting an orchestra. If the player is an accomplished musician, he can make the instrument produce a great range of effects. To be sure, poor organists are all too common in the churches; but what they need is not more organ lessons but more knowledge of music in general. Age does not deteriorate the performance of the organist—nor of the orchestra conductor—as it does the performance of all other musicians. Many outstanding organists and conductors are well past seventy.

The organ, then, is a splendid instrument for study; but the advice to the parent is simple: Let the child first become fairly proficient on the piano.

The electronic

The electronic organ, because of its convenient size, has been used in nearly all funeral chapels, in small churches, lodges, and night clubs. The variety of installations indicates the versatility of the instrument. In the home it is still a novelty instrument and an expensive one. Although secondhand instruments may sometimes be had for six hundred dollars, a new one will cost two or three times that amount. However, they are inexpensive to operate and maintain. Since there is practically no music written especially for the electronic organ, it uses almost entirely music written for the pipe organ or for almost any other instrument. Any pianist can quickly learn to adapt himself to the new instrument. His chief problem is to learn to arrange his music. This requires a good ear and some imagination. The process of arranging usually takes place right at the keyboard and is a large part of the fun of playing the instrument. The variety of tone color which may be had on even the smallest of these instruments is astonishing. Yet musicians in general dislike them, and, paradoxically, because they find them monotonous. The most interesting thing about the electronic is the rapidity with which they have developed in their short life. It is certain that a few more years will bring a greatly improved instrument.

THE HARP

There is no reason why the harp should be classified with the piano and organ except that it is a multi-stringed instrument. It should be in a class by itself, for it is the most individualistic of all instruments. And in no wise is it an easy instrument to play. On the other hand, no instrument enjoys greater prestige than the harp, and even a rank beginner attracts attention and is programed alongside

Prestige

advanced performers on other instruments. The very novelty of the harp makes it attractive. Players are always in demand for the orchestra and many small ensembles include a harp. Although the literature written exclusively for the harp is comparatively limited, the harpist can play much of the music written for piano and other instruments. The enormous attraction of the harp, to children, is its size and spectacular appearance.

Age to begin

The harp is played with the thumb and first three fingers of each hand. Although some of the strings are colored to differentiate them, it remains difficult to find the correct strings quickly, and wrong notes are plentiful from the hands of the beginner. But as soon as the player can provide the correct tones, the charm of the instrument captivates the popular audience, even where content and interpretation are lacking. A child may begin lessons as soon as his hands are large enough and strong enough to pluck the strings easily. Twelve years of age is about as early as is practical.

Cost

The harp, however, pays for its easy prestige by being the most expensive and the most awkward of all instruments to transport. Perhaps this is why it is so rare. Few harps can be procured under a thousand dollars, and there are not many secondhand instruments available. Since harps are scarce, a player always must carry his own instrument. This involves the expense of a transportation truck, insurance and wear and tear, and the inconveniences of delays, keys to get into the building, etc. Although the harp is provided with a sturdy trunk for transportation sooner or later it must go back to the factory for repairs. Merely replacing broken strings may run as high as twenty-five dollars a year. The harpist, however, does his own tuning. Indeed, this is one of the first difficulties which the beginning harpist must overcome.

No teacher

Obviously, the practical difficulties of studying the harp are numerous. Indeed, in many parts of the country it is difficult even to find a teacher, and harpists often travel to a bigger town every other week or so for instruction. No one should undertake the harp without the firm conviction that he wants to play it. Once he has mastered the instrument, the harpist never loses his enthusiasm or devotion.

HOW CAN THE PARENT HELP

Keep the piano tuned.

Ask to have music played.

Provide sightreading material.

Get new music.

Provide occasions for the child to play.

Play and sing together.

Play duets.

VIII

the string instruments

THERE ARE FOUR SERIOUS MEMBERS OF THE string family—the *violin,* or *fiddle,* as its devotees fondly call it, the viola, the cello, or *violoncello,* to use its full title, and the bass, also known as *string bass* or *bull fiddle.* They all have many qualities in common—particularly the violin and viola, but, apart from these two, the player does not change from one to the other without considerable difficulty. Though strings are the heart of the orchestra they have no place in the brass band; but the string bass is sometimes used in the concert band indoors. Nevertheless, the music written for the strings alone is greater and finer than all the music written for bands.

THE VIOLIN

In the orchestra

Most important, certainly, is the violin. The orchestra, which uses only two or three trombones and two or three trumpets, requires twenty or thirty violins. In the concert orchestra they are divided into first and second violins. School orchestras sometimes provide easier parts for third and fourth violins. The same instrument plays any of the parts.

With this great demand for strings the beginning violinist soon finds a place in the school orchestra, even though it be at the last stand. Gradually he works himself forward toward the first stand. Although the second violin parts are generally easier than the first, there is no disgrace in being classified in the second section. As in the jigsaw puzzle each piece, no matter how small, is important.

A good orchestra director always puts some of his better players in the second section, to maintain balance. The young player will probably advance more rapidly in this section than in the first. Some school orchestra directors place all new members in the second section to await their turn in the section of their choice. Some children prefer to play the second part, which lies less frequently in the higher positions.

In small ensembles

The violin is equally important in the small ensembles, such as trios, quartets, and quintets. Of these, by far the outstanding is the quartet—the *string quartet,* composed of two violins, viola, and cello. It would be difficult to exaggerate the prestige and importance of this combination. Almost without exception, every great composer has written some of his masterpieces for the string quartet. The players who have once tasted the delights of quartet playing give it a devotion which often seems fanatical. And among adults it ranks first of all musical combinations as a social acitivity and cultural interest. There are few experiences in all the arts which offer as much to the accomplished amateur.

Literature

The solo literature, too, for violin is inexhaustible. Both with and without the piano, compositions and arrangements are plentiful for any mood or occasion. Moreover, the violin can play directly from the piano score or from vocal music, the hymn book, or the popular song book. As soon as he has mastered the first position on the four strings, the young violinist can take on anything in the singer's range. The violin is a versatile instrument.

Difficulty

The difficulty of the violin, and it is a difficult instrument to play well, is that the fingers must be placed very accurately on the strings to produce the correct pitch. The smallest error brings the sour notes that identify the beginner. But it is not just the fingers of the left hand, which play on the strings, that are important; the right bow arm requires fully as much attention as the left. It is the inexperienced right arm that causes the raucous scratchings, so characteristic of the first weeks on the fiddle.

Since both arms are equally important, there is no

Left-handed players

such thing as a left-handed violinist. The only justification for reversing a violinist's playing position would be the loss of a finger on the left hand, which would then be unable to finger the strings but might still be able to manipulate the bow successfully.

Prestige

The violinist's prestige varies greatly in different localities and in different schools. Among musicians he is ranked at the very top. However, in communities where jazz and parade bands set the standard, the violin is as popular as a scholar at Monte Carlo. The parent should be happy indeed if the child chooses the violin; but it must be realized that only in the better public schools today is the musical standard such as to give encouragement to the string player.

Age to begin

No instrument has produced as many child prodigies as the violin. Lessons may begin earlier on the violin than on any other instrument. Many a normal child has begun lessons at the age of three; and here the advantage of an early start cannot be denied. This should not be interpreted to signify that all children should begin lessons at this age, nor that older children should be discouraged from undertaking the instrument. Many an adult in the fifties has started violin lessons for the first time and made an enjoyable success of it. But when the child begins at a very early age, he learns to manipulate the violin and bow in much the same way that he learns to manipulate his vocal cords in talking. The violin becomes almost a part of him, and it becomes as natural for him to play the violin as to talk. Usable instruments may be had in three-quarters-size, half-size, quarter-size, and even one-eighth-size, for very small children. They are no more expensive than full-size instruments; but of course there is not a great range of choice. It is not difficult for the child to shift to a larger one as he grows up. Consequently, it is practical to begin the violin at any age.

Cost

The cost of a violin varies enormously. They may be had from the twenty-five-dollar price asked by the mail-order houses to the thousands of dollars bid for fine old Italian instruments. Violins do not deteriorate in value unless they are abused. Consequently, violinists often change their instrument, selling the old one for as much or more than they paid for it and buying a new one whose tone pleases them better. In selecting an instrument for a beginner, make sure that the pegs turn easily to enable the child to tune his instrument himself, but not too easily, or they will not stay in place after tuning. New strings, rosin, and rehairing the bow make up the annual upkeep cost of the violin, which comes to about ten dollars. Thus, it is relatively an inexpensive instrument. Considering the results available, there is probably no greater bargain in the entire field of music.

THE VIOLA

Almost no one ever starts to play the viola before he has played the violin. The viola is only three or

Similar to violin

four inches larger than the violin and uses the same system of fingering and the same technique. It is really the alto of the violin family. The chief difference is that the violin reads from the treble clef, 𝄞, and the viola reads from the alto clef, 𝄡. This is no trick at all for any violinist who has studied long enough to be comfortably at home in the third position. The fingering for the third position on the violin is the same as the fingering for the first position on the viola. The transition seldom takes more than a few days and is sometimes accomplished in a single hour. No teacher is necessary to supervise the change. Thereafter, any lessons taken on the viola will have an equally good effect on the violin, and vice versa. It can thus be seen that the two instruments are closely related.

Literature

Almost everything that has been said about the violin can be said about the viola, except that the literature for solo viola is quite limited. Even so, much more has been written for the viola than for any of the brass instruments. But the viola is valuable chiefly as an ensemble instrument. The viola player is a much sought-after member of the string quartet, and there is always a shortage of viola players in the orchestra. Since the viola parts are not as difficult as the violin parts, many a violinist can gain entrance to an orchestra or quartet as a viola player who would not be considered as a violinist. The prestige of the viola player is the result of scarcity.

Prestige

Cost The cost and upkeep of a viola are about the same as that for a violin. Fewer cheap models are made, but otherwise the investment will cost about the same. As stated above, however, few people begin with the viola—they transfer to it by choice, after they have had a year or more of lessons on the violin.

THE CELLO

Difficulty The cello is easier to learn than the violin because the strings are so much longer that the same degree of accuracy is not required to play the instrument in tune. Also the cello parts do not move as fast as the violin parts and there are long sections for cello with easy, repeated notes. This does not mean, however, that a cellist may not spend a lifetime perfecting his playing; but the beginner will be admitted to the orchestra—and the string quartet—sooner on the cello than on the viola or violin.

Also, the cellist does not suffer so much from lack of practice as the violinist, again owing to the fact that his finger intervals are not so fine. It is a splendid instrument for older people to take up. Often children who have become proficient on the piano take up cello as a secondary instrument so that they may play in the orchestra. The cello plays in the bass clef, and since this is the clef the pianist uses for his left hand, he finds no difficulty reading the music. The cello also uses the tenor clef and the treble clef, but this usage does not come till the more difficult music is encountered. Few instruments pay as quick musical dividends as the cello.

Literature

The literature for the cello is also very attractive. In addition to the very enjoyable parts in quartet and orchestra, there are sonatas for cello and piano and solos for cello alone in sufficient quantity to keep even the most industrious cellist busy an entire lifetime. The cellist arrives at a satisfactory tone more quickly than do most other players and soon gets satisfaction from his own playing.

Size

The disadvantages of the cello are its huge size and the difficulty of finding a good teacher. A violin teacher can also teach the cello, but at a handicap. And nothing whatsoever can be done about the size of the instrument. Even the three-quarters and half-size cellos made for young players are bulky to carry and subject to expensive damage in transportation. Cellists do not seem to mind their bulky instrument and treat the inconvenience as a good subject for jokes.

Age to begin

Because of its size and the necessary long stretches in playing, most children do not begin the cello until they are about ready for high school. However, some children have begun with success as early as three, using, of course, the half-size cello. A knowledge of piano is of great value to the beginning cellist.

Cost

The cello has the same incidental expenses of the other string instruments—strings, bow rehairing, rosin, etc. Fifteen dollars a year will usually take care of these. The chief cost hazard is breakage, and the child is frequently not to blame. The big soft bags cellos are carried in give little protection. It is a wonder they are not damaged more frequently.

The original cost of a cello is only slightly above that of the violin. Second-hand instruments are easily located, and an instrument adequate for a beginner can usually be procured for under a hundred dollars. Since it can probably be sold for the same price, the investment is not a great one.

All in all, the cello is a good choice as a child's instrument. It does not require the devotion of the piano or violin and yet it has a fine literature and is a much sought instrument.

THE STRING BASS

The string bass has a most formidable appearance but is quite a passive instrument. Since there is practically no literature for the bass alone, it depends upon the orchestra and concert band for its prestige. A man-sized instrument, on that account it attracts the interest of many a young adolescent, besides being an easy instrument to play—probably the easiest in the entire orchestra. This is not because the big stretches of the long strings are easy to manipulate, but because the parts written for the bass are slow-moving and uncomplicated. To be sure, some com-

Difficulty

posers do write terrific passages for the bass section, but these are usually doubled by the cellos, which can render them more fluently; and the school conductor does not expect his basses to display such virtuosity.

Age to begin

Obviously, this is no instrument for a small child. Not only must the youngster be of good size, but his fingers must be very strong to be able to stop the huge strings. Given the proper physique, a high-school youngster will quickly master the instrument sufficiently to take his place in the school orchestra or band. The dance band has recently welcomed the string bass to its midst, giving the instrument a prestige such as it has never enjoyed before.

Easy to keep in practice

Because of the enormous string length, the fine accuracy demanded in the higher stringed instruments is not so essential on the bass. Consequently, it takes much less practice to keep in form. Many an adult continues to play string bass in some amateur orchestra as his chief avocation.

Transportation

It is unnecessary to point out that the great disadvantage of the instrument is its size. Most players do not even attempt to transport their instrument back and forth but leave it where they must play it and go there for practice. The better high-school orchestras own basses for the children to use, and the child either practices on the school bass or buys his own instrument and keeps it at home, using the school bass in the orchestra. There are trunks available for the string basses, but they then must be moved by a regular transfer company. Ordinarily the bass is kept in a close-fitting cloth bag.

Cost The cost of the string bass is surprisingly high. Although battered second-hand instruments may sometimes be had for very little money, a good bass, either new or second-hand, will cost over three hundred dollars. As with other string instruments, however, the investment can be regained at any time, if the instrument has not been abused. The full-sized bass is enormous and is seldom used in high-school organizations. Even symphony orchestras frequently use the seven-eighths size. They are also to be had in the three-quarters size and sometimes even in five-eighths and one-half size. The smaller sizes are not noticeably cheaper. The upkeep of the bass is also unusually large. Although strings, rosin, and rehairing the bow will not likely run over twenty dollars a year, the huge curved expanses of wood in the instrument are liable to crack and become unglued. If left unrepaired such damages will quickly lower the value of the instrument. The violin repairman in cities of over fifty thousand will be able to do the job; but it does add considerably to the cost of playing the bass viol.

In closing, a word should be said about the great musical satisfaction which comes from playing the string bass in a good orchestra, where the powerful roots of all the most sonorous chords are given to the bass section. The physical exercise and the gratification of feeling oneself the foundation of the entire tonal structure are ample reward for the inconveniences of taming the "bull fiddle."

HOW CAN THE PARENT HELP

Provide strings. Always have a spare on hand for each string.

Provide rosin, mute, tuners—these are all inexpensive and do much to keep the young violinist happy.

Do not scold the child for scratches and nicks that may appear on the instrument. They are inevitable in the early stages of learning. But—

Try to avoid having the instrument or bow laid down in a chair. Sooner or later someone will sit on it. Have a *convenient* place to lay it down. Keep it easily accessible but out of danger.

Do not allow other children to handle the instrument, unless they know how to play it.

Provide a good music rack and keep it conveniently placed for use.

Help the child to tune the instrument. If the pegs stick, put soap on them. If they slip, put chalk dust on them. If they cause too much trouble, take the instrument to a violin repair man; for a small sum he will make them turn easily and yet hold firmly.

Play accompaniments.

Play and sing together.

Arrange for duets and other combinations of players.

IX

the wood-wind instruments

THIS SECOND GROUP OF THE ORCHESTRA SOON MAY have to change its name, since the wood winds seem to be in process of becoming metal. Already the wood flute is obsolete and the clarinets used in public schools are more often metal than wood. The oboe and the bassoon, however, continue to be made of wood.

These four are the principal instruments in the wood-wind group, but there are several others in less frequent use: the piccolo, English horn, alto clarinet, bass clarinet, and double bassoon. These latter are never studied as beginning instruments but are undertaken after testing more familiar relatives.

Difficulty

All the wind instruments are easy to learn so far as fingering is concerned; the difficulty lies in the blowing. The beginner wants to concentrate on the fingering, because it looks as if that was all that was necessary to play the instrument. Were that the case, every pupil would be an accomplished performer well within a year. Each instrument has eight or nine holes to be covered by the fingers and perhaps twice as many keys and rings to be manipulated. But the fingers lie always over the same holes, and the keys are always played by the same finger. There are two or three ways of playing the same note, but that is nothing compared to the hundreds of complicated positions of the hands which pianists and violinists use in playing their many tones and chords. The difficulty of the wind instruments is in the embouchure—the control of the muscles around the mouth, which makes it possible to get the right tone, if the fingers are playing correctly.

Embouchure

It is a mistaken idea of laymen that all that is necessary is to put down the right fingers and blow and the right tone will come forth. Such is not the case at all. The right fingers may be down, but only if the lips are correctly shaped and held just firmly enough in that position, and the right amount of air is blown at the right pressure, will the right tone come forth. True, anyone can put an instrument to his lips and give a sudden whoof of air and get some sort of a tone; but this tone is of no use in music, because the pitch is not accurate enough and the tone quality is not under control.

This control of the embouchure can be easily observed in whistling, where we vary the pitch by changing the shape of our lips and tongue almost imperceptibly. Consider the amount of practice it would take to gain an efficiency in whistling at all comparable to the nicety demanded in orchestral instruments. This will help you realize all that must go into the development of a good embouchure, and you will understand why it is the chief problem of the student on a wood-wind instrument.

There is always the struggle between the pupil, who wants to practice new fingerings with the firm conviction that he can play anything as soon as he has mastered them, and the teacher, who is anxious that the pupil practice long, slow notes, which will strengthen the embouchure and give him the necessary control.

Keeping in practice

Because of the necessity of keeping his embouchure in good condition, the wind player gets out of practice much faster than string and keyboard player. If he does not touch his instrument for two weeks, he will play badly. If he lets it go a little longer, he will not even have the strength to play more than a short time. On this account the wood winds are not practical for adults, who can give only irregular time to practice. The justification for a child's undertaking a wind instrument should be the use he will make of it during his public school and college years. There is little likelihood of his using it in later life.

THE CLARINET

Diffi-culty

By far the most common of the wood winds is the clarinet. It is the easiest to play; consequently, there are many more players, good, bad, and indifferent, on the clarinet than on any other wood wind. Yet there never seem to be enough. Though the orchestra uses only two or three, the band calls for solo parts and first, second, and third clarinets, each part using several players. The band director is always searching for more clarinets. The clarinet is also interesting as a solo instrument. All the popular melodies are arranged for clarinet and piano, and there are many fine sonatas written for this combination by some of the finest composers. There is enough literature to challenge even the most ambitious player.

Litera-ture

Trans-position

The clarinet is a transposing instrument. When the clarinetist sees a C on the staff and plays that C, the sound which comes forth is a B flat, if he has a B-flat clarinet. It is A, if he has an A clarinet. And it is E flat, if he has an E-flat clarinet. Thus, if he has a B-flat instrument, his part always sounds one whole tone lower than written. Therefore, his part must be written one whole tone higher than it is to sound. Consequently, a clarinet cannot read music from a piano score and play it with the piano—he will always be one tone too low.

This may seem a foolish arrangement. The reason is historical, and we must accept the situation as we find it. If the player wishes to read from piano and vocal and violin music, he can learn the fingering as if he were playing on a C instrument. This is no more difficult than learning to read in two clefs, as every pianist and cellist does, nor than learning to finger in seven positions, as every string player does. However it is not ordinarily required of the clarinet players, and few are willing to spend the few hours necessary for its accomplishment.

E-flat clarinet

A Clarinet

The E-flat clarinet is a much smaller instrument and is used almost exclusively in large bands. The A clarinet is but slightly longer than the B-flat and is used only in orchestral work for music written in keys that are not easy for the B-flat instrument. If the key is inconvenient for the B-flat clarinet, it will be convenient for the A, and vice versa. However, the B-flat is always the instrument used by the beginner.

Fingering systems

The arrangement of keys, and consequently the fingering, varies slightly on different clarinets. There are two main systems: the old *Albert system* and the modern *Boehm system.* In America the Boehm system is almost universally preferred. The additional keys or rings sometimes added to Boehm clarinets are of no importance to the beginner. He should learn on the straight Boehm-system B-flat clarinet.

Cost

The cost of a clarinet ranges from fifty to three hundred dollars. The cheapest are made of plastic; the finest of wood. The ones most used by school children are metal, to avoid cracking or chipping and joints becoming loose and leaky. They may be had at a very reasonable price. There are always second-hand instruments available. If these need reconditioning, they may prove more expensive than a new instrument.

Adjusting and repadding a clarinet costs between ten and twenty dollars. This is necessary every two or three years with just ordinary usage. A crude test of the working condition of an instrument may be made by stopping all holes with the fingers and covering the bell with the palm of the hand. By blowing hard in the instrument the air can be heard escaping if there are leaks. A crack in a clarinet makes it nearly worthless, no matter how cleverly it has been filled. The crack almost invariably reopens. Although it is much harder to play on a cheap instrument, it is questionable if too big an investment should be made for the beginner. The beginner is very hard on his instrument. He grabs it in such a way as to twist the finely adjusted keys out of line: he forgets to swab it out and keep it dry, and the excess saliva which inevitably escapes from inexperienced lips soaks the pads which then dry out of shape. It is best to buy a moderately priced instrument and later turn it in for a really fine instrument, when the child has shown a permanent interest and can appreciate a good clarinet.

Reeds

The clarinet is a single-reed instrument. The reed is a thin piece of bamboo, three inches long and half an inch wide, which is fastened onto the underside of the mouthpiece by a removable metal band. The vibration of the reed produces the tone. Obviously, the reed is an important part of the instrument. Their cost is the chief item of expense in the upkeep of the clarinet. They cost only fifteen cents apiece, but they break or split very easily. Reeds are like spectacles; one has to learn how to protect them. The beginner seldom wears out a reed; he splits it by brushing it against his clothing or breaks it as he lays it down. Eventually he learns to keep the mouthpiece cap on, when not playing.

It is essential not only that there be a reed on the instrument but that the reed be suited to the player. This is *very* important. Two or three dollars spent in finding the right reed for the child will do more to help his progress than several lessons. The beginner needs a soft reed, and gradually, as his embouchure is strengthened, he requires a stiffer one. If the reed is too stiff, he does not have the strength to play it; if the reed is too soft, he cannot get a good tone. As stated above, a large part of learning to play the clarinet consists in strengthening the embouchure so that a stiff reed can be used which will give a good tone. The wise parent will buy a dozen reeds at a time and allow the child to try them out and select the one best suited to him. The others should then be carefully put away. The reed that is too stiff today may be just right in another two weeks. But if the reeds are left in the clarinet case, they are likely to be spoiled through carelessness before they are used. A reed gradually softens through use, particularly if it is not wiped dry after each practice period. Thus the reeds continually get softer as the pupil's strengthened embouchure demands stiffer reeds. The parent can help in no greater way than by keeping an adequate supply of reeds at hand. A very fine clarinetist, when asked how he found a satisfactory reed, replied, "I buy a gross of them at a time and hope that I may find *one* which will suit me."

Prestige

Because of its humble and unostentatious appearance the clarinet has never enjoyed great prestige with adolescents. When it behaves well, it has a soft, sweet tone that is not at all sensational; when it misbehaves, it squawks in a most ridiculous fashion. Children select it because they are sure of a place in the band, or because they can transfer from the clarinet to some other reed instrument, or because it is easy to carry, or because it is more easily obtainable than most instruments. Often, however, they become fascinated by its range of musical expression and study it intensively enough to become splendid performers with access to some very fine literature.

Age to begin

Ten years of age is probably as young as it is profitable to undertake this instrument, since the fingers must be large enough to cover the holes and the embouchure strong enough to control the reed.

Alto clarinet

The alto clarinet is larger than the A clarinet, is shaped like a saxophone, and is a transposing instrument, usually in E-flat. The bass clarinet is still larger and the bell curves upward much like a saxophone; it is a B-flat instrument, exactly one octave lower than the familiar clarinet. Both of these instru-

Bass clarinet

ments are fingered and played exactly like the B-flat clarinet. A player who has learned on one can change to the other without great difficulty. They are occasional members of both band and orchestra.

THE FLUTE

The flute is a fast-moving instrument and requires a quick player. It has a place in both orchestra and band and is often used in small ensembles. The early composers wrote fine sonatas for flute and piano. Since the flute is non-transposing it can read music from the piano score or play many pieces written for the violin, though the lowest five notes of the violin cannot be played on the flute. Consequently, there is plenty of good literature for the flute.

The flute is not a reed instrument. The tone is produced by directing a rift of air from the lips directly onto the edge of the opening in the mouthpiece at just the right angle to cause the column of air in the flute to start vibrating. The process is the same as that by which one gets a tone by blowing on the edge of a bottle. Since this requires even finer control than a reed instrument, the flute is more difficult to play than the clarinet. However, children of twelve seem to master the instrument without too great difficulty and some high school children are splendid performers. Since it is not necessary to bite the instrument and consequently less strength is required in the embouchure, flute players are more likely to use their instrument when they are adults.

A flute under a hundred dollars is a bargain; a good one will cost over two hundred. However, the cost of upkeep is next to nothing. Every few years it may need new pads and slight adjusting, but otherwise the initial cost is the final cost. Second-hand instruments are all right if they are not cracked and are in correct pitch. The new ones are all metal and cannot be injured except by inexcusable abuse.

There are two systems of fingering available for the flute, depending upon the arrangement of rings and keys on the instrument. The old *Meyer* system is being replaced in all public schools today by the new *Boehm* system. Eventually a child will insist upon a Boehm system, so it is wise to buy it in the first place.

The fact that it is sometimes difficult to find a teacher of flute is an indication of the comparative rarity of the instrument and it is this that gives it prestige. A flutist is always welcomed and respected. He gets enjoyable and challenging parts to play.

Piccolo

The piccolo, the smallest instrument in the orchestra, is nothing less than a small flute, sounding just one octave higher. The fingering is the same, the reading is the same; only a little practice is necessary for the flutist to learn the piccolo. It costs slightly more and has a far smaller literature but it is a flashy member of a football band and comes in at the climactic points of big orchestral works. Usually the man who plays piccolo in the orchestra also plays the third flute parts. The piccolo is never undertaken until the player has mastered the flute. By then he is in a position to know whether or not the smaller instrument is feasible.

THE OBOE

The oboe is one of the most difficult instruments to learn and should not be undertaken unless a child can be counted on to stick out a rather discouraging period of early instruction. Part of the trouble is the cost of a good instrument. Most children have to learn on inferior instruments, which increase the difficulties. There are two major systems of fingering for the oboe—the old *military system* and the *conservatory* or *improved conservatory*. The fingering system is not as well standardized as on other instruments; that is, there is greater variety in the number and arrangement of keys and rings. Some form of the conservatory system is preferred today. A new conservatory oboe will cost over three hundred dollars, and there are few second-hand ones available. It is not surprising that oboe players are few!

Moreover, the oboe is a double-reed instrument. Its reed resembles a soda-fountain straw about three inches long, crushed flat at the end which the player holds in his mouth. The instrument is of black wood, slightly smaller than the clarinet, and the reed comes straight out from the end. This reed is made from two thin narrow pieces of cane bound together by fine thread. Its extreme sensitiveness is the source of most of the oboist's unhappy moments. It is always too wet or too dry, too soft or too stiff. Before any orchestra concert you can see the oboist, his reed stuck in his mouth like a cigarette, trying to get it into just the right condition for his first entrance. When the time comes for the orchestra to tune up, the oboe gives the pitch and the entire orchestra acknowledges his preeminence.

The reeds cost two or three dollars apiece. Many players learn to make them themselves exactly as they desire. Plastic reeds are made for school children. They do not break nor dry out so easily; but the professionals say their tone can never be completely satisfactory. They may be practical, however, in the early lesson stages, when there is so much to be learned all at one time.

The oboe is often undertaken by a clarinetist, and the ability to handle the single-reed clarinet is an enormous advantage in learning the oboe. Otherwise, twelve years is about as early as it is advisable to undertake the oboe. The instrument appeals to adults, perhaps because of the very fine solo parts it has in the orchestra.

Although it cannot be played with a marching band, because of the sensitivity of the reed, the oboe is essential to a concert band. However, it is in the large orchestra that the oboe comes into its own. There it has some of the finest solos written, and even in rather unimportant passage work its tart tone quality sounds out in clear line through the entire orchestra. It is indeed a gratifying instrument to play! It also appears in small ensembles, and there is a limited literature for oboe and piano or oboe alone. The instrument is suited to a player with personality.

English horn

The English horn is the alto of the double-reed family. About six inches longer than the oboe, it has a small, curved metal tube, into which the double reed is fitted, projecting from its upper end. The lower end has a bulb about the size of a lemon in place of the usual bell. Its tone resembles the oboe's but the range is a fifth lower. It is a transposing instrument, sounding a fifth below the written note. Although not a regularly established member of either orchestra or band, the English horn frequently has essential solo parts to play. Obviously, it is not an instrument for an unsophisticated beginner. It is usually played by oboe players, who seem to have little difficulty in making the shift.

THE BASSOON

The bassoon is the bass of the wood-wind group. It is a double-reed instrument but not nearly so difficult to play as the oboe or English horn. Although it is essential to a complete orchestra and is a member of the concert band, it seldom plays outside these groups. Some of the parts written for it are exceedingly difficult, but most of the material it is asked to play can be handled by a player of average ability.

It is impossible to enumerate all the systems of fingering for the bassoon. The system generally is selected by the teacher; but the school bassoonist takes what he can get. The size of the instrument necessitates a large hand and few undertake it before the age of thirteen or fourteen. The cost of the instrument varies greatly according to its condition and model. A prospective player will do well if he finds one under two hundred dollars. Usually the school furnishes the bassoon and is happy to find a player.

The huge instrument with its comical shape, looking like two or three sticks of wood bound together, with a white ring on top, is matched by its comical tone. Its tart, incisive tone quality and its ability to sputter and do gymnastic skips make it the clown of the orchestra. Its novelty attracts school children and many want to take it up on that account. It is a justifiable choice for a boy or girl who wants an instrument to play during high school and college. Often pianists adopt it as a secondary instrument. Any youngster who really works at it will be able to play in the orchestra in less than a year's time.

Double bassoon

The double bassoon is just one octave lower than the bassoon. It has one more coil and usually involves some metal in its structure. It is used on certain occasions in the orchestra and concert band, but is not essential to either group.

FLUTE AND PICCOLO

TUBA

BASSOON

ENGLISH HORN

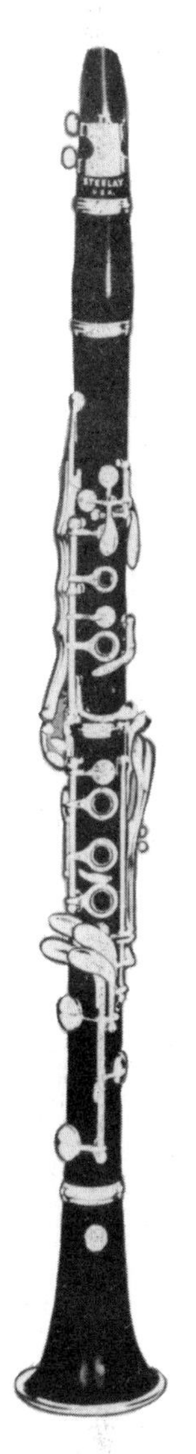

B♭ CLARINET

OBOE

TROMBONE

CITIES SERVICE BAND

NBC SYMPHONY ORCHESTRA UNDER ARTURO TOSCANINI

VIOLIN

VIOLA

CELLO

STRING BASS

TRUMPET
CORNET
ALTO SAX

Before leaving the wood winds, mention should be made of the chief ensemble group of this section, known as the *wood-wind quintet.* It is composed of a flute, an oboe, a clarinet, a bassoon, and one brass instrument—the French horn. Much music has been written for this combination.

HOW CAN THE PARENT HELP

Provide a good convenient music rack.

Encourage swabbing out after each use of the instrument. A good swab for a clarinet can be made by tying a lady's handkerchief to one end of a string and a fishing-line sinker or some small weight to the other.

Do not allow other children to hold the instrument. Even with the best of intentions they may bend some of the sensitive keys slightly out of place.

Buy music of various sorts for fun.

Accompany the child or occasionally provide an accompanist.

For the clarinet: Buy reeds—plenty of them. Allow the child to try them all out and select *one;* put the others away and do not bring them out until he wants to select another. If the reeds are left easily accessible, most of them will be spoiled or lost before they are used. It sometimes helps to draw pencil lines on the back of the reeds to indicate whether they are the right stiffness, or just a little too hard or too soft, etc.

Let the child know that you enjoy listening to him play.

X

the brass instruments

Diffi-culty

AS A GROUP THE BRASS INSTRUMENTS ARE EASIER to play than the strings or wood winds. They have a special appeal to the young adolescent because they are bright and shiny and make a big noise. With the exception of the French horn they are easy to play, because the parts written for them are comparatively simple. Perhaps on the same account, there is not very much written for them to play outside of the band and orchestra. The solos arranged for the brasses from piano and vocal literature are seldom more than pretty or commonplace tunes. There is no real solo brass literature.

Keep-ing in prac-tice

Although the brasses are easy to learn, this is offset by the necessity for continuous practice. A trumpet player in one of the big symphony orchestras put it epigrammatically: "If I miss a single day's practice, I can tell it; if I miss two days' practice, my director can tell it; and if I miss three days' practice, my entire audience can tell it." Because of this the brass instruments seldom function at all after the child leaves school with its daily band or orchestra practice. The absence of any literature which would interest a serious adult fosters the attitude that brasses are juvenile instruments. Adults use them only in lodge bands or American Legion festivities.

Cost

Because the brasses are made of a good hard metal, they are less liable to damage than the wooden instruments. Only the trombone with its fragile slide is easily harmed. Consequently, the initial cost of the brass instrument is the sole cost. Moreover, the brasses do not require a reed or any accessory. The tone is caused by the vibration of the air column, which is begun by the vibration of the player's lips.

Embouchure

Thus here, as in the wood winds, the lips and embouchure are of the first importance. Indeed, the learning process is chiefly a matter of strengthening and attaining control of the embouchure. Therefore, while the young student is impatient to play more notes and new tunes, the teacher must insist on slow practice and long sustained tones, to develop the strength in the embouchure necessary to good tone.

Versatility

Since all of the brasses, with the exception of the trombone, have the same three valves and are fingered approximately the same, it is possible for a player to shift from one to another with little inconvenience. The embouchure differs between them sufficiently for an advanced player to avoid playing an unfamiliar instrument, lest it spoil his embouchure for his own instrument; but most high-school players will shift from one to another with surprising versatility.

Transposition

The brasses which read from the treble clef are transposing instruments. That is, when they play C it sounds B flat, or E flat, or F, according to the key of the instrument. Consequently, these instruments cannot play from a piano score or from vocal music and be in tune with the piano. It is possible, however, for players to learn to read their notation as if they were all C instruments, and then they can read directly from the piano score. This is not too difficult a task. If the instrument sounds B flat when they play C, this is a transposition downward of one full step. Therefore, to make the instrument play like a C instrument, they must simply finger one full step higher. At first attempt, this seems confusing, and most players give up before they have given it a fair trial. But with just three or four hours' practice at this new fingering, they will find it as easy as the fingering they learned originally. The littlest child at the piano learns to read one clef in the right hand, with E on the first line, and another clef in the left hand, with G on the first line; and he plays them both at the same time. The problem confronting the brass player is not nearly so difficult.

Prestige

The prestige which the different brasses enjoy varies with the age of the children. In general, the more difficult the instrument, the greater its prestige. In early adolescence, the trumpet is the preferred instrument.

THE TRUMPET AND CORNET

The popularity of the trumpet is due largely to the fact that it seems such a virile instrument. The player stands up straight, holds his head high, and blasts forth a tone in heroic style. Moreover, in the brass bands it is the trumpet or cornet which carries the main melody.

There is little difference between trumpet and cornet, so far as the beginner is concerned, although he often thinks there is. Actually the trumpet is a slightly longer instrument and its tube is cylindrical throughout almost its entire length, whereas the cornet tube grows gradually larger throughout most of its length. There are also differences in the mouthpiece and in the shape of the bell. Manufacturers, however, have created models which combine the characteristics of the two in such a complex variety that it is often impossible to say what each instrument is. The manufacturer's names for them have no significance.

The symphony orchestras employ real trumpets; the outdoor brass bands generally prefer the cornet. The pure trumpet is more difficult to play, but other factors might enter in to contradict this generalization. For school use the choice is immaterial. Only an advanced player can tell the difference in the playing. In the following discussion, everything said of the trumpet is equally true of the cornet.

The trumpet is a transposing instrument in B flat, that is, when it plays C, it sounds B flat. Consequently, the trumpeter cannot play with the piano from the piano score unless he learns to read his instrument as a C instrument.

Some children begin the trumpet as early as six years of age; but the lips are so weak that progress may be very difficult. Twelve years seems a good age to begin.

A fine trumpet costs around two hundred dollars, but second-hand ones are always available at a great range of price. If the valves come up quickly, as quickly as the finger can come up, the instrument will probably do for a beginner.

Since there are only two places for trumpets, in the orchestra a player, unless he is very good, may not get in. In the band, trumpets and cornets are much more numerous. Even here, however, players are so numerous that at the university only the better ones get in. High-school music directors complain of our excess of trumpets and cornets.

The bugle

The bugle is really nothing more than a cornet without valves. Bugles are usually in the key of F or G. Regardless of their key, they are played like the cornet but without the valves. Of course, they can only sound the notes used in the bugle calls; but there is no finer preparation for the cornet or trumpet than practice on a bugle. Where parents feel that the interest in a trumpet is not likely to continue long enough to justify buying an instrument, they may well compromise by buying a good bugle, which can be had for around ten dollars, new. It will delight any youngster and help him make up his mind about starting a more complicated instrument. The boy-scout bugle is satisfactory .

THE TROMBONE

The trombone is much like a trumpet, an octave lower. Instead of valves it uses a slide to lengthen the tube and get the various pitches; but its general shape and manner of playing is the same. The *tenor* trombone is the familiar instrument.

When it plays from the treble clef, it is a B-flat instrument, and the written part looks just like a trumpet part. Of course, it sounds an octave and one full step lower than the written note. However, the trombone also reads from the bass clef, and then it is non-transposing; that is, it sounds the same tone that it reads. Therefore, in the bass clef it can read from piano score while in the treble clef it cannot. This is just one more idiosyncrasy in musical tradition. The young player today must choose between the two clefs and select his music accordingly or learn to read both clefs. The latter is certainly the advisable procedure and is necessary in advanced trombone playing.

Since manipulating the trombone slide requires a fairly long arm, few children under fourteen are able to play the instrument. It is not difficult to learn to play well enough for average school use, but advanced playing requires as much practice as any wind instrument. It is considered a very manly instrument and is always popular with the boys.

A good instrument costs over two hundred dollars, but it is usually possible to get a satisfactory second-hand instrument for less than half that price. In selecting a second-hand instrument, make sure that the slide works easily and evenly. To test the instrument, put the thumbs over both open ends of the slide mechanism, without attaching it to the bell of the horn. (This is the separation that is always made to put the trombone in its case). Then let gravity pull the slide down. If it falls slowly and evenly, the trombone is in good playing condition. If it falls rapidly, there is leakage and the instrument will be hard to play. If it does not fall at all, the slide is stuck and the repair bill may be considerable. The slide is easily damaged; and a satisfactory repair can seldom be made without sending it to the factory.

The orchestra uses three trombones, one of them a bass trombone; the band uses many more. However, there are seldom enough trombones to meet the demand and the trombonist is welcomed in the organization of his choice.

Bass trombone

The bass trombone is a slightly larger instrument with a slightly larger bell. It takes a long arm to play comfortably and is usually undertaken by the older boys who have grown up on the regular tenor trombone.

THE BARITONE HORN

The baritone horn is similar to a trombone in range and tone quality but looks nothing like it. It has a large bell, and the player holds it in front of him or at an angle under his left arm. He plays it with three valves like a trumpet. Like the trombone it reads either in the treble clef as a transposing instrument or in the bass clef as a non-transposing instrument. It is a B-flat instrument.

The orchestra never uses a baritone horn, unless as a substitute for some missing instrument. But the band has a very enjoyable part for the baritone, where it plays the main counter-melody and is a highly respected instrument.

Although rather bulky the instrument is not as awkward to manage as it appears. It is easy to learn and easy to play. Its size is the only thing that limits the age at which a child may undertake it. A large twelve-year-old can manage.

The baritone horn is not as expensive as one might anticipate from its size. A new one will cost around two hundred dollars and second-hand ones may be had quite reasonably.

Euphonium

The euphonium is a particular model of baritone. It has a second bell, much smaller than the main bell, which serves to give better quality to the higher tones. Its mechanism is so similar to the baritone that no baritone player has difficulty playing the euphonium.

TUBA AND BASS HORN

The bass horns comprise an entire family in themselves. They are built in many sizes and keys, but since they play from the bass clef, they are considered non-transposing instruments. The player therefore cannot shift from one to the other without learning a new system of fingering. Since the parts written for them nearly always move slowly, bass players generally do not hesitate to take up an instrument in a different key and figure out the fingering as they play. Regardless of the size, they all play the same part; the selection of sizes is to give variety of tone quality. The price varies with the size of the instrument.

The orchestra uses only the big tuba.—It is the biggest horn in the orchestra and when the player holds it in his lap it completely hides him. It is the most expensive of the models and has the finest tone quality. It is preferred in the band but is seldom used because it is too bulky to be played on the march. Only husky youths should undertake these big horns.

The helicon bass is made for use on the march. Its huge coil of tubing encircles the player and rests on his shoulder. There are three popular sizes; the single B-flat, which has the same range as the baritone horn; the E-flat, a fifth lower and correspondingly larger; and the double B-flat, which is still lower and with a double coil of tubing to give it the necessary length. It is surprising, however, how easily a sixteen-year-old boy will carry even one of the largest of these instruments on parade.

The preferred model today, is the sousaphone. This is similar to the helicon bass but its bell can be turned in any direction, like a stovepipe ventilator, thus permitting the sound to be directed toward the front of the band when on the march. Sousaphones also come in the three keys—the single B-flat, the E-flat, and the double B-flat.

THE MELLOPHONE OR ALTO HORN

This is the alto of the cornet family and comes in several different models, all transposing in the key of E flat. They read from the treble clef. The alto is sometimes shaped like an oversized cornet and is played in a similar position. Sometimes it is built like a small baritone horn and is held with the bell up, directly in front of the player's chest. Its more modern version is the mellophone, with a circular coil of tubing and a wide flaring bell. It is held under the player's left arm. The mellophone is the most expensive model, but a satisfactory instrument can be secured for between fifty and a hundred and fifty dollars. Regardless of the model, the instrument has the same three valves and can be easily played by any cornet player. It is by far the easiest of the brasses to play, but the part given to it in the band is very uninteresting. As a result, the instrument has little prestige and is all too often played by cornet players not good enough to get into the band on their own instrument. In the orchestra the instrument is used as a substitute for the French horn when no French horns are available. The beginner on the mellophone, however, has the advantage that he can transfer to a French horn and thus profit by this training.

THE FRENCH HORN

The French horn is the aristocrat of the brasses. Its beautiful, flexible tone has made it a favorite with composers and public alike. It is by far the most difficult to play and the first horn is one of the highest-paid members of the symphony orchestra. Mere possession of an instrument gives caste to the fortunate young owner.

The difficulty of the instrument results from the length of the thin tube used to produce the many tones in its enormous range. The tubing is wound in a complicated coil which is held at the player's right side. There are three rotary valves, different in construction but accomplishing the same purpose as the three valves on the other brasses. These valves, however, are played by the left hand. The construction of the instrument makes it possible for the French horn to play notes from the bottom of the trombone range to the top of the easy trumpet range. So much desired is its tone quality, that composers give it more than its share of solos, and it also gets countermelodies and much fill-in work. In short, it is decidedly overworked. In big symphony orchestras the first horn player is given an assistant, who sits beside him and plays the less important material, so that the solo horn player may save his lip for more important passages.

A full orchestra calls for four horns, and the band for at least as many. So scarce are players on this golden instrument that conductors are always looking for another horn player. This is the only brass instrument, moreover, which commands a solid place in small ensemble groups. The horn is a regular member of the so-called wood-wind quintet, and numbers have been written for it in combination with other instruments. There is almost no solo literature for it, however.

The French horn, or just *horn,* as it is popularly known, is an F instrument. It reads in the treble clef, except on rare occasions, and when it plays C it sounds F. But music for horns is written for various keys, and consequently most horns are outfitted with several crooks which can be slid into place on the instrument and change it to an E-flat or a C or a low B-flat horn. Furthermore, the solo horn player is asked to play in the higher range so much of the time that a horn is specially built for this purpose, known as a *double horn.* It has an extra crook built right into the instrument, so that when an extra valve is pressed, it becomes a high-B-flat horn. This enables the player to reach the high tones more easily and with better tone quality. Prized by every young aspirant of the horn, this model costs around four hundred dollars. Other models come lower, but at best a horn is not a cheap instrument.

Although the horn is definitely the most difficult of the brass instruments, a child has no more difficulty with it than does the adult. A twelve-year-old can reach the valves easily and often learns with great rapidity. Horn players like their instrument so well they never change to another. The French horn is indeed the aristocrat of the brasses.

HOW CAN THE PARENT HELP

Help to keep the valves in good—in *perfect*—working condition. Ask the teacher's advice as to how to do this.

Provide a good solid music rack and keep it handy.

Remove the mouthpiece every time the instrument is laid down; this discourages other children from meddling.

Provide mutes and polish; they add to the pride a child takes in his instrument.

Help carry the instrument, if it is large. Transportation can become as great a chore as practicing.

If the instrument is a transposing instrument, encourage the child to learn it also as a C instrument from the very start. He gets much enjoyment and practice from playing off a piano or vocal score.

Encourage the child to join the band. Band parts are easier than those in orchestra. Many children are timid about making the first connection with an organization.

Buy band parts for the child to practice at home.

Play accompaniments to his solos.

Arrange for combinations of instruments, when possible. Nothing will do more to induce interest and practice.

Get enough music for fun—not just what is needed for lessons.

XI

the saxophones and percussions

THERE IS NO REASON FOR GROUPING THE SAXOphones and percussions together except that they both are so badly played. This is probably because they are so easy that novices often present themselves as accomplished performers long before they have acquired any musical sense. A good saxophone well played is a fine instrument but exceedingly rare. Because a complete scale can be played with almost no practice, the saxophone has become a noisy toy which, as usually played, obliterates the musical efforts of other instruments.

Organizations

Actually there is no place for the saxophone in the orchestra, but school directors often use it to fill in missing bassoon, cello, oboe or other parts. The director is never happy about the situation, but it is better than omitting the parts entirely. In the band the saxophones have a regular place, alto and tenor being favored.

The reason the saxophone has not been accepted as a member of the regular orchestra is because it is a hybrid instrument. Being made of brass it has too brassy a quality to fit in with the wood winds. But it uses a reed and consequently has too reedy a quality to blend in with the brasses.

Various models

The saxophone family is numerous. There is the somewhat rare *high-C melody,* a tiny instrument with a shrill voice, looking for all the world like a meerschaum pipe. Sometimes it is built like a tin horn—a straight tube. Next comes the *B-flat soprano,* slightly larger than the meerschaum pipe model. Parts are written for it in the large band scores, but it is not essential. The *E-flat alto,* which comes next, has long been the most popular member of the saxophone family. The player holds it easily under his left arm and has good parts both in concert band and dance band. The *C melody* is just perceptibly larger than the alto. It has declined from its former popularity because bands provide no part for it. The *B-flat tenor,* next down the scale, and slightly larger than the C melody is one of the most respected of the entire family because of its fine tone, which has some resemblance to the cello tone. It is given interesting parts in the band and is generally present in the dance band. Finally comes the *E-flat baritone.* This instrument almost touches the floor when the player is seated. Though not as important as the alto and the tenor, it generally has a part to play. In fact, the *B-flat soprano,* the *E-flat alto,* the *B-flat tenor,* and the

E-flat baritone make up the conventional saxophone quartet. A *B-flat bass* saxophone is sometimes seen in dance-band combinations. It is a monster.

Transposition

All except the high-C melody are transposing instruments. The C melody was manufactured to play from the piano score. All of the family, however, read from the same treble clef but sound from a step lower in the case of the B-flat soprano, to two octaves and a step lower in the case of the B-flat bass. The fingering is the same for all, and a player can change with ease from one to the other. Indeed it is the adolescent saxophone player's dream to sit in the dance band behind a rack holding the entire family of saxophones and play one after the other without a break.

Cost

The cost of the saxophones is out of all proportion to their usefulness—from one hundred and fifty dollars upward, according to size and ornamentation. But second-hand ones are available at very reasonable prices. Reeds have to be bought and occasionally a pad needs repair, involving an upkeep of between ten and twenty dollars a year.

Reeds

The saxophone reed is large and rather soft even for the beginner. Consequently, a child can play a saxophone as soon as his fingers are big enough to reach the keys—probably about ten years old for the E-flat alto. There is no great difficulty in keeping in practice; the instrument makes no great demands on the muscles of the embouchure. Adults play the instrument as easily as do children. Usually, however, the player deserts his instrument for some other as soon as he becomes interested in serious music.

THE PERCUSSIONS

Timpani, kettle drums, pedal timpani, bass drum, snare drums, field drums, orchestral snares, cymbals, triangle, tambourine, wood block, tom-tom, tam-tam, castanets, xylophone, glockenspiel, marimba, bells, chimes, siren, whistles, and others too numerous to mention comprise the percussion section. Few own them all, but all young players aspire to possess the entire inventory.

Difficulty The instruments are not difficult to play for those with an easy feeling for rhythm, but others find it almost hopeless. The difficulty is coming in on time and keeping in time. The player without this ability is an exasperation to any conductor. Many a pianist with a good sense of rhythm can play the percussions more satisfactorily after an hour of practice than the average beginner after two years. To determine whether or not a child has this feel for rhythm, just get him some drum sticks and let him practice.

Many of the finest percussion players have never had lessons but have apprenticed themselves into the business rather gradually. A good sense of rhythm and a feeling for the music are the chief requisites. The one technical item which requires any considerable practice is the roll on the snare drum. A few lessons with a good drummer are essential to learn *how* this is done; long practice is then necessary to master it. Although the list of instruments is long, the same rolls are used on nearly all of them; the player does not study and practice each instrument separately.

Timpani

The *timpani* (also spelled *timpany* and *tympani*) are popularly known as the kettle drums. Every symphony orchestra must have at least a pair of these and a third is desirable. For school use the pedal timpani are preferred for their ease in tuning. Since each drum can be tuned to only one note at a time, it is often necessary for the timpani player to retune his instruments to a new pitch several times during a number. Easy tuning therefore increases his efficiency in the orchestra. Each school usually owns a pair of timpani, which cost around three hundred dollars new. Whether or not it is advisable for the beginner to own kettle drums should be decided only after consulting the school director. It is usually wise for the child to buy something which the school does not have, so that the percussion section may be more complete. On the other hand, this sometimes restricts the child to the instrument which he brings, while some other child, who owns no instrument, is allowed to play the school timpani. The timpani player is the most desired position in the percussion section being the only one who has a part in all serious orchestra music.

The *bass drum* is too well known to need de-

Bass drum

scription. The greater the diameter of the drum, the less incisive the tone will be. The greater the depth of the drum, the more resonant the tone will be. Children tend to select the drum which looks bigger, the one with the greater diameter, but the better choice is the one with the most resonant tone. A satisfactory bass drum may be had for between one and two hundred dollars. A cradle to hold the drum off the floor is essential. If the drum is to be used in dance work, a pedal attachment will be required to beat it. For band and orchestra work an ordinary beater is sufficient.

Snare drum

The *snare drum*, or *orchestral snare*, is generally the first request of the aspiring young drummer. It is the shallow metal drum which rests at an angle on a metal rack and is played with two wooden sticks. This is the best instrument for practice of the difficult roll. One may be bought for thirty dollars up, and second-hand ones are always usable. This drum is used occasionally in the symphony orchestra and is the spice of the dance band.

Field drum

The *field drum* is similar to the orchestral snare but is made of wood and is much deeper—the deeper the more resonant the tone. It is used with the marching band and sometimes indoors. It costs about the same as the smaller snare drum.

Cymbals

The *cymbals* are the big metal disks which are crashed together for huge accents. They are best played by a single player who plays nothing else; but the youthful bass drummer likes to have one fastened to his drum, so that he can hold the other in his hand and play both drum and cymbals at the same time. With the dance band one cymbal is generally suspended from a metal rack, and the player hits it with his bass-drum beater or with his snare stick or with some other stick shaped to suit the occasion. Thus there is quite a variety of cymbals available. A satisfactory one can be had for only a few dollars. The drum set, which most young drummers ask for at Christmas, includes the bass drum, the orchestral snare, a pair of cymbals, and the accessory sticks, beaters, and racks.

Triangle

The *triangle* is nothing but a metal bar bent into the shape of a triangle and open at one corner. It can be had in various sizes and costs only a couple of dollars.

Tambourine

The *tambourine* is the shallow little drum with chattering metal disks fitted in its sides, which is shaken or struck for effects, chiefly in Spanish music. It costs two or three dollars.

Block

The *wood block* is a hollow piece of wood played upon by the snare-drum sticks to imitate horses galloping, etc. It costs a couple of dollars.

Tom-tom

The *tom-tom* is a hollow-sounding drum; it is sometimes called a *tam-tam*. The tam-tam is a metal drum or deep-sounding cymbal.

Castanets

Castanets are the two little shell-shaped pieces of wood which are made to click within the palm of the hand. A pair costs a couple of dollars.

The *bells, xylophone, glockenspiel,* and *marimba*

Bells Xylophone Glockenspiel Marimba

constitute a class in themselves. They are a series of metal or wooden bars arranged somewhat like the black and white keys of a piano and played upon by two or more mallets. A part for them in orchestra or band is very rare; but they have a great fascination for children. They are expensive instruments. They are not easy to play but can be learned successfully without instruction. They seldom serve any other purpose than novelty.

Many other accessories are used by the percussion section; their need and use vary with the particular musical group with which the player is connected.

HOW CAN THE PARENT HELP

Provide racks for music and the necessary paraphernalia.

Encourage the young player to get into a group.

Provide plenty of music.

Encourage the saxophone players to learn to read from piano copy.

Provide a proper place for practice to avoid disturbing the family and neighbors and encourage uninhibited practice.

XII

casual instruments

THERE IS CONSIDERABLE MISUNDERSTANDING, even among older children and adults, concerning those occasional instruments that have found no place in orchestras or bands but are used here and there or have a passing vogue—guitars, mandolins, banjos, ukuleles, accordions, zithers, etc. A single enthusiast coming into a community may revive the fad, and start every youngster clamoring to possess and play the new instrument.

There is nothing harmful in learning to play these instruments. There are no *bad* instruments. It merely seems a pity that all the time spent on them would have been better spent on an instrument which can sustain the player's interest and offer him some real music literature. No literature worth mentioning is available for any of these instruments. At best the players can perform a few popular airs or folk tunes in a desultory manner alone, or in a group. However, the fun of learning the instrument often justifies the investment in time and money.

The only musically significant gain from such instruments is the development of the ear, since they are usually learned by ear. The player may have an elementary chart to help him with the notation or fingering, but he trusts to his ear to tell whether or not he is playing correctly. This should be true on every instrument, but all too often the teacher of the standard instrument teaches it without any reference to musical effect. Haphazard self-instruction on any toy instrument is preferable to this; at least the child will not learn to dislike music.

Guitar

In Spain the *guitar* is an instrument of considerable importance, rising even to concert rank. In America it has been little more than a plaything. It is larger than a violin and is played by plucking with the fingers. The *steel guitar*, a smaller variation of this instrument, became popular in this country a few decades ago. It has been used chiefly for oriental music with simple melodies which glide from one note to another.

Mandolin

The *mandolin* is about the size of a violin but has a larger, pear-shaped body. It is played by strumming with a quill or plectrum. Half a century ago it was the rage in all colleges, and mandolin clubs toured the country. Today it is occasionally brought down from the attic and tuned anew to play *Sweet Adeline*.

Banjo

The *banjo* has long been associated with the black-faced minstrel. It looks like a small snare drum with a long neck or fingerboard attached to it. Today a larger model known as the *tenor banjo* is considered an essential part of the dance band. It is strummed like the guitar.

Ukulele

The *ukulele* is probably the best known of these strummed instruments today. It is little more than a toy but ornate models may cost as much as a hundred dollars.

All of the above-named instruments can play simple melodies with a comfortable chord accompaniment underneath. In the hands of artists they become serious musical instruments capable of presenting standard concert repertoire; but for the most part they are little more than musical toys.

Accordion

Much more consistent popularity has been enjoyed by the *accordion* or *squeeze-box*. With its ability to keep a lively melody and a continuous organlike accompaniment going at the same time, it holds the interest of the performer sometimes for years of casual practice. Our grandparents danced to its music, and in some localities today classes of twenty or thirty accordions play ensemble. Many people of foreign extraction will pay as much for an accordion as for a piano. The cost varies with the number of sections which will unfold and thus give greater length to the instrument when it is fully extended, and also with the amount of pearl inlay and silverplated keys.

The *piano-accordion* is so called for its addition of a small piano keyboard, on which the melody is played with the right hand. Either of these two instruments is also confusingly called a *concertina*.

Zither

The *zither* is another instrument which enjoys a certain continuous popularity. It has the advantage of a string for each melody note, arranged in sequence like the white keys of a piano. Thus it is simple to pick out tunes, and children find it a fascinating novelty.

The *autoharp* is a zither to which bars with dampers attached have been added, making it possible to play harp-like chords by sweeping the fingers across the strings.

Mouth organ

Although the *mouth organ*, or *mouth harp*, or *harmonica*, as it is variously called, is usually considered a plaything, it is actually just as serious an instrument as many of those named above. In the bigger cities where there is a large foreign population, it is not unusual to find ensembles of mouth organs practicing regularly in the community centers or in the recreation parks during the summer months. Good instruments may be bought for from one to five dollars, and since they may be carried in a boy's pocket, they are a fine investment in recreation.

Ocarina

The *ocarina*, or *sweet potato*, has the same advantage. As its nickname implies, it has the shape of a sweet potato with small holes at various points to be covered by the fingers. It is simple to play and is often used in combination with two or three mouth organs. If this is desired, care must be taken to secure an ocarina in the same key as the mouth organs.

Recorder

Of quite a different social character is the *recorder*. This simple, flute-like instrument, played by blowing in one end, was popular three and four centuries ago. It then occupied a position very much like the violin today, and quartets of various sized recorders were as common as a table of bridge today. There is a current revival of such ensembles, not only among children but serious-minded adults interested in reproducing the music of the early composers. This instrument, a forerunner of the modern flute, is so easy to play that a person scarcely has to learn; he simply begins playing.

There are various sizes, the most important of which are the soprano, alto, tenor, and bass. They range in price, according to size and material, from three or four dollars for the smallest, plastic instrument to fifty or more for the large wooden models. Although there are alternative fingering systems, the eight or nine holes which the fingers cover are sufficiently simple in arrangement so that a player may transfer with ease from one instrument to another. There is plenty of music available to make this a challenging instrument; and publishing companies are rapidly reprinting the best of the seventeenth- and eighteenth-century compositions for this instrument, both solo and in groups. The instruments are also used in the schools to interest children in music in situations which do not permit the organization of a regular orchestra.

This by no means completes the catalogue of casual or novelty instruments. The fad of a new or an old instrument is likely to come in whenever an enthusiastic player moves into the neighborhood or some manufacturer thinks he can start a new hobby.

One class of instruments used in school, however, calls for separate mention. These are the pre-orchestral instruments. They have various names and structures, but they are all planned to prepare the child for study of a more serious instrument. Thus the *violette* is a simplification of the violin; the *clarinette* a simplification of the clarinet, etc. They have a use as teaching devices but cannot be considered as serious instruments. If the local teacher needs them in his method of teaching, the school will probably provide them, but most teachers of the standard instruments consider them a waste of time, a subterfuge of poor teachers.

On the other hand, some elementary-school teachers in the earlier grades use these instruments very cleverly as more or less exploratory instruments. They encourage the child to take home one instrument after another, much as he might take home library books. to discover which intrigues him most. Thus the child may bring home a xylophone one day, a tambourine the next, followed in rapid succession by drums, cymbals, and instruments without name or pedigree. This is good fun, if the family can stand it, and encourages the child to listen critically to the various types of sound which come forth. It is a healthy, normal step in the selection of a serious instrument.

The playing of any instrument which requires the child to listen to pitch and tone quality is certainly time well spent. At this level the small investment in such an instrument is well justified. The problem is to decide when the child has graduated from this elementary level in music and is ready to take on a more serious instrument which will really challenge his musical ability.

HOW CAN THE PARENT HELP

Be sympathetic with these various investigatory interests, but avoid too serious emphasis.

XIII

voice

LIKE THE OTHER ARTS, MUSIC HAS ITS CONTRADICTIONS and superstitions. The confusion is worst in vocal music. There is scarcely a statement about the voice made by one vocal teacher that will not be denied by another.

A good voice

What is a good voice? The answer is—the one people like to hear. Listen to any one radio station throughout an entire day and it will become apparent that no set standard for vocal quality exists. Even performers and recordings selected by experts at the radio studio and the record workshop show no uniformity. For a consistent opinion you will have to restrict yourself to a voice teacher or vocal director, but it is likely to be a narrow and arbitrary opinion.

Classification

When it comes to classifying a voice, the confusion is just as great. It is not at all uncommon, even among concert artists, to find a singer who for years has been trained as a tenor to be discovered by another teacher to be a baritone, or vice versa. Of course, it may be that the voice does change; in fact, its quality should change as the voice is developed. But the confusion can seldom be so explained.

Age to begin

Similarly, on the age at which vocal training may profitably begin, there is great divergence of opinion. Some voice teachers frown on formal voice instruction until eighteen or twenty when the voice, male or female, has settled. Others advise lessons immediately, regardless of age. The extent to which the possibility of private gain may influence the judgment must be evaluated by the parent.

Injury to the voice

Membership in a children's choir is cautioned against by many a vocal expert. The parent is told that intensive singing at this age ruins the voice and makes it unlikely that the child will be able to sing at all as an adult. It is certainly true that a fanatical voice teacher or director can ruin a child's voice, or the voice of an adult, for that matter, by insisting upon intensive artificial technique of tone production; but it is absurd to presume that ordinary natural usage of a voice can do it any injury, even when rendering difficult vocal music. The yelling and shouting which any group of adolescents does at every baseball or football game should be conclusive evidence that the vocal mechanism is not the fragile organ which many voice teachers would have us believe. Were the voice so easily injured, there would be no adult singers today. The proportion of adult choir singers who sang in children's choirs refutes the notion that children's choirs ruin the voice.

Placing the voice

The situation is clarified when we analyze the task of the voice instructor. First, he must *place the voice* and so train it that the tone quality will be the best available from that voice; second, he must teach the vocal literature. The training of the voice is usually the chief concern in the vocal studio. The means by which this is accomplished vary so greatly from teacher to teacher that the parent can only judge between different methods by the product turned out. If a teacher has produced a number of fine voices, the likelihood is that he will continue to do so.

Literature

Unfortunately, most voice teachers pay little attention to the acquisition of vocal literature. Years and years are often spent on trifling songs of no musical value, all the emphasis going to tone quality or vocal gymnastics. As a result many vocalists, after years of serious study, know almost nothing about music. They have just arrived at the point *musically* where the instrumental beginner is the day he starts.

This unfortunate situation is partly due to the nature of vocal music, where words are important, frequently the only important part of the piece. The singer is encouraged to give all his attention to the tone quality and trust to the words to furnish the rest of the appeal of the song. The proportion of worthless material published for voice is therefore enormous.

The good literature for voice, however, is also enormous. An impressive number of composers have written master works for solo voice. And as much fine choral literature can be found as in the instrumental field. The nineteenth century, however, was decidedly a period of experimentation with and emphasis upon instrumental music. It was during this century that the big orchestras were developed and the great symphonies were written. Choral music in that period tended to imitate orchestral music to its own detriment. At the present time we are witnessing a reaction in the choral field. Good choral conductors are appearing and choruses are seeking an effective style of their own.

Accompanist

The vocal field, then, is a challenging one. Many paths of development are open. It is for the individual singer to choose. Regardless of what is done with the voice, however, all vocal teachers agree that some knowledge of the piano is desirable. The student who can play piano fairly well learns to read vocal music easily; few other voice students ever learn to read well. Moreover, the vocalist who must always depend upon an accompanist for practice is at a decided disadvantage. The accompaniment usually gives the cue to the memorization of a song and the piano is certain to affect the harmonic and melodic feeling of the vocal line.

Organizations

Membership in church choir, school chorus, or glee club is highly desirable. Any voice teacher who objects to such participation on the grounds that it will injure the voice or interfere with the instruction is open to suspicion. Participation in a good choral group is certainly more valuable than instruction with such a bigot.

The more singing a person can do, the better. The autobiographies of our great singers all attest to the enormous amount of natural, spontaneous singing they did as children. We can do no better than follow their example. The best advice is: Sing and enjoy it.

HOW CAN THE PARENT HELP

Do not tolerate ridicule by anyone; nothing is more discouraging to a voice student.

Sing as a family.

Encourage singing when the young folks gather together.

Have the right music ready.

Play the accompaniments or arrange to have an accompanist present occasionally.

If you cannot play the piano, learn to play enough for accompaniment. It is not difficult to accompany, if you do it from the beginning.

Encourage the singer to learn the piano so that he can play his own accompaniments. Singers who play the piano are nearly always better readers.

XIV

the selection of a teacher

Parent as teacher

THE PARENT IS THE BEST TEACHER. THE PARent always objects that the child will not work for him, that he knows him too well, that he will pay more heed to an outsider, etc. But there are counter arguments. The teacher cannot possibly know the child as well as the parent. The lessons cannot come at such convenient times, nor as frequently—if frequency is desirable. And it must be remembered that the money spent for lessons can be spent for recordings, instruments, music, or other items which will greatly increase the understanding of music.

We must admit that this role of teacher is one of the most difficult roles the parent may ever undertake. It is easier if the parent begins before the child has entered school and adopted a formal attitude toward the teacher. It becomes easier again when the child is in the later years of high school and turns to the parent for information in some special field. That it can be done very successfully is proved by the large number of superior music students entering the university who were taught entirely by a parent or at least had their early music lessons with their parent.

Music at its best is an intimate experience of mutual enjoyment. Like intimate speech and etiquette, it is best learned from the parent. Most of the parent's apprehension in this situation comes from a fear of the untried. Let him set a regular time for the lesson and take on the more formal air of a teacher, and many of the difficulties will disappear. Write down what is to be practiced and use a formal checking system as the various tasks are done. This avoids the procrastination and evasion which otherwise may be encountered. Set a reward for the accomplishment of a certain piece. Arrange that it be played for someone—an uncle or an aunt or a grandparent. Play duets. They take much time; but how could time be better spent? Even though the parent be an experienced teacher, regularity will remain the greatest difficulty. It is so easy to put off the lessons till another time. The youngster has not practiced; he will not be so tired another time; company has arrived. The rule should be to act as if this were a formal lesson for which a good price has been paid. It CAN be done.

However, usually the parent cannot perform this

role and the teacher must be selected. There is no simple rule for distinguishing the good teacher from the incompetent. The best we can do is to call attention to some of the indications of good and bad teaching.

Certification

Certification of teachers is often suggested as a solution to the dilemma of parents who must make a selection and have no other basis. Certification, however, has not made it easier for us to select our family doctor. In a field like music, where there is almost no measure of good teaching, it would probably be neither helpful nor fair. It is highly questionable if certification of public-school music teachers has improved the situation. It has established a standard and eliminated some undesirables, but it has also excluded some of the most desirable teachers.

Scholarships

Nor are the "part scholarships" and "talent certificates" which are offered to young students to be taken seriously. There is usually a catch, and the parent will find himself paying more for the "part scholarship" than the entire fee should be. This type of charlatanry is not as common as it used to be; but many smaller music schools still offer lessons with their "master teachers" at "reduced" prices, higher than the actual value received.

Many paths

There is no one royal road to performance on any musical instrument. Any teacher claiming to have the fastest, or the best, or the only way to success in music should be avoided. It indicates a narrow point of view. Similarly suspect is the teacher who on taking an advanced pupil insists that all the work done by the first teacher was wrong and must be done over again. A search for a third teacher had better be made immediately.

Gadgets Beware, too, of the teacher who gets the children interested in gadgets. Playing blocks, colored cards, pictures of note ideas, number systems, fancy metronomes—they may be good entertainment but have little to do with music. They are adopted as a crutch by teachers incompetent to teach the music itself. At the best, they waste time which the pupil would gladly spend on music; at the worst, they lead the child to think that music is a childish thing.

Ear playing Most dangerous is the policy of not allowing the child to play by ear. In previous generations teachers made note reading their sole objective. Since ear playing seemed to interfere with this objective they forbade it. We now know that ear playing helps fast reading. Some teachers, however, still forbid the child to attempt to play anything by ear—the most musical way of learning a piece.

Ear playing is simply singing with an instrument instead of with the voice. The few children who do not learn to sing with their voices are monotones. Babies begin to experiment with their vocal cords almost as soon as they are born, and they continue until they are well along in adolescence. Since the piano or violin or any other instrument is not an intimate part of the child's anatomy like the vocal cords, we are conscious when the child begins experimenting with his instrument, that is, when he begins to play by ear. However, the more he can play by ear, the easier he can learn to read music. A familiar parallel, once more, is in the case of reading English. The more words a child has in his vocabulary, the easier it is for him to read advanced literature. It is as absurd to restrain a child in playing by ear as to restrain him in talking. The policy of constraining a child in such normal activity belongs to the period when children were "to be seen and not heard."

Inversely, it follows that a teacher who makes extensive use of the ear in teaching is an effective teacher. It should be obvious that good teaching of music necessarily involves the ear in as active a manner as possible. It is not unusual today to find a teacher who encourages the pupil to play by ear, showing him new chords to use and suggesting pieces to work on.

Harmony

The use of harmony during the lessons nearly always indicates a good teacher. He is teaching not only the instrument but a sensitivity to music itself. The unprepared teacher does not know enough harmony to be able to use it in his teaching.

Personality

Because of his or her long and intimate association with the child the music teacher often becomes a great influence in the shaping of ideals. A warped personality in the teacher is likely to develop a warped personality in the child. Unfortunately, many disappointed aspirants for the concert stage turn to teaching as a means of making a living. Because of their one-sided ambition and training, these teachers are likely to be fanatics. The teacher should be a normal person.

Boys generally prefer a man for a teacher, but a sympathetic woman whom the boy likes will overcome this preference.

Former students

After all, selecting a teacher is not unlike selecting a good business house of any sort; the business which has turned out the best product is the best concern. This does not mean that the best performer indicates the best teaching, unless performance is the sole aim of the parent. Rather it means that the pupil who enjoys his music most, who feels it as an art experience and wants to continue study, is the product of the best teacher. When you know such a child, you can feel safe in choosing his teacher for your child.

Cost

The cost of lessons varies greatly in different communities. The highest-priced teacher is probably not the best for beginners. Many mediocre teachers have learned that they can gain prestige by charging a big fee. But even a teacher who is well prepared, if he has had extensive concert experience, may prefer advanced students and may not be a good choice for a beginner. Nevertheless some of the finest pianists enjoy working with young children. It is a matter of personality.

The charge for lessons should be commensurate with the amount of time the teacher has spent in preparation for teaching. If the time spent at music lessons and at college equals that which a doctor spends in his preparation, the rate for time should be the same. Usually music lessons are not so expensive, because of the oversupply of music teachers.

Frequency of lessons

If lessons are too expensive, it is usually possible to arrange for a lesson every other week. This is probably not advisable for children, unless the parent can provide some sort of stimulus and check-up between lessons. On the contrary, it is preferable for the small child to take two lessons a week. Where the steps are small, there must be more of them.

Free lessons

Free lessons are never good. Whether the pupil does not value them and consequently does not practice, or whether the teacher's indifferent attitude discounts the effectiveness of his lessons, is not certain. In any case good results from free lessons are decidedly the exception. Under this generalization is included the "free" term of lessons which comes with the purchase of an instrument. Obviously, such an offer is made to sell the instrument; there is little reason to suppose the lessons will be worth anything.

The term of lessons

Some teachers charge for lessons in advance. Many irresponsible parents arrange for lessons and then do not send the child or send him irregularly. Since the teacher's time is reserved for this particular pupil, he cannot sell it to another, and consequently he expects to be paid for it, regardless. Most teachers, however, will arrange to make up the lesson, if notified in advance that the pupil will not come. Many teachers, particularly in the larger cities, avoid all the unpleasantness of arranging for lessons and their irregularities by teaching at a music school or conservatory. Here the lessons are always contracted for in semesters or terms and no irregularities are tolerated. Since there is as much diversity among schools of music as there is among private teachers, they are no guarantee of good instruction. It all depends upon the individual teacher.

XV

the relation of parent to teacher

THE PARENT IS OFTEN THE CHIEF CAUSE OF unsatisfactory music lessons, even when he is trying hard to help. He interferes too much or misunderstands what is to be expected from a private teacher. The following *do's* and *don'ts* should help improve the relationship and indicate the proper etiquette in certain situations.

Do not expect the teacher to come to the home, unless you pay extra for the lessons.

Do not expect the teacher to give extra time. Good teachers are in great demand and their schedule allows no time between lessons.

Do not expect the teacher to converse before or after lessons. Conversation before reduces the amount of time the teacher can devote to your child's lesson. Afterwards, it makes the teacher's succeeding lessons late. When it is necessary to discuss some matter, make a special appointment when the teacher has free time.

Avoid canceling a lesson. If you have reserved a certain time, the teacher cannot use it otherwise and has a right to expect payment for it. If your reason is that the child has not practiced, you merely encourage him in avoiding further practice. Lack of practice indicates that the teacher needs more time to influence the child, not less. Moreover by such an attitude, you indicate unmistakably to the child that the music lessons are to be regarded as of secondary importance. Do not expect any great devotion to practice after this, unless you have one of those rare children who is going to learn music *in spite of you.*

Do not stay in the room during the lesson, unless the teacher requests it. Out of politeness most teachers will say they do not mind; but the teacher is rare indeed who does not prefer to be alone with the pupil. The child probably offers alibis that influence the parent, but the teacher understands this and can cope with the situation much better alone. The music lesson is an occasion where the child develops his personality and self-assurance; this possibility is removed when the parent is present. The child may find the music lessons a trial when he has to try to please both teacher and parent at the same time.

Do not demand a certain piece to be taught. If the child wants the piece or is willing to oblige you by learning it, a request or suggestion to the teacher is in order; but only the teacher can know whether or not it is advisable at a particular time.

Do not interfere with the child's choice of what he would like to practice. He learns fastest when he is practicing the thing he prefers. If his choice seems a bad one, discuss it with the teacher.

Do not play the child's piece for him, unless the teacher requests it. The child copies it very quickly, and you may completely mislead the teacher. However, if you cannot play the piece nearly as well as the child, he may be amused and elated. No harm will then be done.

Now for the positive part of the parent's activity.

Get the pupil to his lesson on time. If he is late, you should expect a shorter lesson. However, the same significance does not attach to the teacher's lateness. Talkative parents and extra minutes of explanation to some previous pupil may disorder the teacher's schedule. The teacher must continue to give full time to each pupil and has no opportunity to recover lost time.

With some younger pupils, the teacher wants the parent to write down the assignment and help the child to remember it. Always send the assignment sheet or book back for the next lesson. If it is a sheet of paper, clip it to the front of a book, so that it will be easy to find.

Buy the music on time. It is usually possible to phone a music shop and have the music mailed to you. Every child looks forward to new music; it is an incentive to enthusiastic practice.

Clear the practice time of competing attractions.

Provide a comfortable and convenient place to practice. Get the right chair and a good music rack or anything else that is necessary. These small details do much to determine whether practicing will be fun or an annoyance.

Avoid coercion in getting the child to begin his practice. He practices best when relaxed. After he gets to his instrument, let him alone.

Convince the child that you enjoy hearing him practice. No one can practice who feels that he is annoying those around him.

Ask the child to play for your entertainment. It is more important that he be convinced that *you* enjoy his music than that he be able to please others.

Accompany him or play duets with him. This always relieves the monotony of practice.

Occasionally bring home some music for the child to read for fun, just as you bring books and magazines into the home in the hope that they will be read.

After considering all that is expected of him, the parent may feel that it is he, who is taking the music lessons. And he is not entirely wrong. Both the blame for failure and the credit for success fall equally upon parent and child.

XVI

class lessons

TWO CENTURIES AGO IT WAS BELIEVED THAT reading and writing and arithmetic were best taught by private tutoring. Only those who were too poor to afford a tutor sent their children to schools. It took almost a hundred years to discover that children learned better in a group than in isolation. But it has taken almost another hundred years for us to realize that children learn music faster in classes than they do in private lessons.

This is because music has not been studied by such large numbers as the regular school subjects, or because music teachers are uninterested in educational theory. Many music teachers still protest that only inferior results can come out of class lessons. These teachers are expert in private tutoring, but probably know nothing of class-teaching procedures. Perhaps, too, they are afraid that the rich mine of private pupils, upon whom they depend for a living, will be exhausted. The old "tutors" were likewise opposed to the "pauper schools."

Class lessons are nowadays frequently organized in connection with the public schools. They are often said to be fine for the beginner but not for the advanced student. This depends entirely upon the teacher. As long as the results continue good, the classes are good. Advanced pupils are being successfully taught in classes, even at virtuoso level.

In selecting a class for lessons, however, the parent should make sure that it is really a class and not just a group of children who sit idle while waiting their turn for brief individual instruction. Many private teachers, incompetent to teach a class, have adopted this procedure and advertise it as a music class. In a true music class every pupil is occupied all the time. Classes will vary from six to twenty or more, according to the ability of the teacher and the equipment available.

The advantages of the class are many. In addition to the lesser cost is the greater amount of time which the child has with the teacher in a class, since class lessons are longer than private lessons. The pupil does considerable actual practicing right under the teacher's eye. There is greater variety of activity in the class lessons and thus the child's interest is held longer and with less fatigue. The children take turns playing at the piano; they practice technical exercises; they discuss correct and incorrect fingering; they watch each other's hand position; they choose between various interpretations; they play duets. There is never a dull moment in a good piano class. Since they are playing together all the time, it becomes second nature to keep together, and they never encounter the same difficulty as private pupils when they first play in an ensemble or accompany someone. Most privately taught pianists never become good accompanists: and the privately taught violin player similarly finds it difficult to fit into an orchestra or a string quartet.

Recital or playing for friends or any other form of performing for others is no ordeal for the class student. He has been playing before others ever since he started on his first piece. But for the private student performance in public is a terrifying ordeal.

Then there is the stimulus of competition. Whether the wish to outdo someone else is desirable or not, it is an inevitable motive and a potent one. There is no stronger incentive to enthusiastic practice, and such competition becomes a greater reality in class where one's rivals are constantly in sight and in action.

Another advantage of the class is the variety of interpretation. In the private lessons the pupil has his own interpretation or is required to take that of the teacher. In the class each youngster who plays a piece gives it a slightly different twist. Through this variety one's own interpretation is developed and enriched.

But the greatest advantage of the class lesson is the opportunity that it offers for the development of the ear. The child's ear is much more active when listening to his own results in comparison with someone else's than when he hears only his own notes. Also in class lessons the teacher often devotes considerable time to regular drill in ear training, for which there is seldom time in private lessons. Many private teachers combine one class lesson each week with one private lesson, to provide time for ear training and ensemble playing. The pupils enjoy such meetings.

It is often objected that the individual pupil does not receive enough attention in class to take care of difficulties that are peculiarly his own. But children are not so different and individualistic as parents often think. There are no more idiosyncrasies in music learning than in mathematical learning. A good teacher can take care of them in any instance. If extra time is needed outside the regular lesson any good teacher will take this time on his own initiative.

The difficulty in class lessons is that the children do not all progress at the same speed. But this is true of all school subjects and happens not to be as bad in music as in arithmetic, for instance. Nevertheless it is a handicap to the ambitious student.

Up to a point a good teacher can cope with this problem by giving the rapidly advancing student extra assignments in music, exercises in transposition, harmony, etc. Eventually it becomes necessary to transfer such a student to another class or arrange for private lessons.

The greatest contribution class lessons have made to music teaching, however, is their social atmosphere. Music lessons have always marked a child as slightly different from the *gang*. He was a *sissy*, a *snob*, just "a little different." Class lessons have completely washed away this attitude. The solitary feeling, so unnatural to a child of school age, is replaced by enthusiastic participation in a group activity. On this account it is perhaps more advantageous to start children in classes than in private lessons. Thus a healthy, enjoyable attitude toward music is ensured.

In determining to use class instruction, however, the parent should remember that class lessons are a comparatively new procedure. They are still in the experimental stage. It requires a more clever teacher to be successful in teaching twenty pupils at a time than to teach one pupil at a time. There are many poorly equipped teachers in the field who talk glibly of methods but know little of music. If, however, a good class can be found, it will be the happiest and most profitable solution of music lessons.

XVII

progress and recitals

Various objectives

IT WOULD BE FINE IF THERE WERE SOME SCALE by which to measure a pupil's progress in music. But standards and objectives are so different that no such measure can be attempted. One teacher seeks to make the pupil a good reader. Another emphasizes interpretation. A third concentrates on technique. Even when teachers agree on the relative importance of one or the other, they will still differ over the emphasis to be placed on them at the beginning. Good teachers will shape their program to suit the needs and ability of the particular student.

Nor are parents any more of a mind as to what they expect. Some parents want their child to be able to play by ear. Some want him to be able to read a little. Most parents say they want him to play "just for his own amusement." Even they, however, will later ask the teacher when the child is going to have something ready to play for people. Obviously, with such diverse objectives, there can be no single scale for measuring success or stages of advancement.

Recitals

The most generally accepted measure of progress is the recital. This gives an advantage to the pupil who is training for performance and works against one who is studying music just for fun. With allowance for variation in objectives, however, the parent may gain some idea of how his child is progressing at these recitals.

Stage fright

Children dread recitals, particularly if they are given in a large public hall with a raised platform or stage, while, at the same time, they thrill at the opportunity to be in the spotlight and gain prestige. The parent may help to allay the fears by suggesting that the recitals are not so important, that everyone forgets sometimes, and that few in the audience will recognize mistakes. Even the fear, however, has some value. It will lead to more intensive preparation.

Organization

Some compelling event like a recital is often necessary to get the child to organize his practice and concentrate on a particular task. In this way the child learns to work toward a faraway goal.

Repetition

Few parents realize, however, the amount of repetition necessary to make sure that a piece of any difficulty will go correctly in recital. The disadvantage of this repetition is that it limits the variety of music which can be studied. Yet, familiarity with basic chordal progressions and melodic patterns are sometimes gained only by the many repetitions stimulated by a coming recital.

Memorization

A necessary part of preparation for a recital is the memorizing of the music. Although time-consuming, this exercise fosters a permanent feeling for music. Just as memorizing poems increases the vocabulary, so memorizing music increases musical facility. The ear then becomes more important than the eye or fingers. Memorization by ear encourages playing by ear and musical understanding. The parent who asks for pieces that have been memorized and almost forgotten will encourage the use of the ear, because the auditory memory lasts longer than either the visual memory or the kinesthetic memory.

Some children rise to the occasion at a recital and surprise even their teacher. Other children experience stage fright and fail to do their best. The parent must make allowances.

In trying to gauge his child's progress, then, a parent will do well to recollect the precise objective in having the child study music. Is that objective being gained? That is the measure of the progress being made—not the excellence of a particular performance. The best over-all index, regardless of all other considerations, is: Does the child enjoy his music?

HOW CAN THE PARENT HELP

Go to the recitals.

Have refreshments or a little party after the recital. Even grown-ups must be helped to relax after performing. It makes a happy occasion out of what is otherwise likely to be an ordeal.

Get a nice scrapbook into which the programs can be pasted.

Ask the child to play his best pieces to you alone, for your enjoyment.

XVIII

musical groups and contests

MEMBERSHIP IN THE ORCHESTRA OR BAND IS THE most frequent incentive of children in their teens to take music lessons. These organizations stimulate them to more enthusiastic practice at home and provide a great amount of practice on the instrument at school. There is a thrill in playing or singing with a large group of other children the same age; the power of the total tonal ensemble seems to belong to each.

Band

The band is the usual objective of children who take to the brasses, but it is considerably overrated as a musical organization. Although the members play together frequently, its music is so simple and so often repeated as to slow the child's musical progress. This is particularly true in the marching bands where the music becomes incidental to the majorettes and the marching convolutions. During the winter the better concert bands work up some programs and give the children a taste of music literature. But even the best literature for the band is restricted almost entirely to transcriptions from original pieces for orchestra or for piano. Nevertheless, the robust nature of the tonal structure appeals strongly to the adolescent; membership in the band is a healthy recreation.

Orchestra With the orchestra, the case is quite different. The string players and most of the good wood-wind players look to the orchestra for the satisfaction of their ambition. The orchestra literature is enormous and of high quality even in pieces for beginners. The director of the orchestra is likely to be a good musician, particularly if he plays one of the wood-wind or string instruments. Although it takes the orchestra longer to prepare a program, the quality of the music studied makes it time well spent.

Ensembles But the finest musical experience for the child is in the small ensemble group such as the string quartet, the trio, the duos, the chamber-music orchestra, the wood-wind quintet. These are not easily organized. The players have to be of about equal musical ability and of a somewhat similar social nature. The music for these groups is both expensive and difficult to find. The school music directors seldom have time to supervise all the groups, which, in their first stages, need considerable guidance and encouragement. Sometimes parents can take over this responsibility, and the group develops in the homes, which is the ideal situation since it encourages continuity after school is over. These groups help fill up the dull summer stretches, when some organized activity is highly desirable. Christmas carols, serenading, family sings—all have strong appeal but usually require the initiation and help of an adult.

Duos

Where it is not practical to form a group, it is always possible to organize duets. There is music available for two of any kind of instrument, and many combinations of two different instruments have been published. For the pianist the most simple ensemble is in accompanying. This is more difficult than it appears to the fellow who is not doing it; but it cannot be taught. Encourage the child; try different compositions; facility can be acquired only by doing it.

Chorus

The choral organizations are numerous—church choirs, school choruses, glee clubs, quartets, etc. They are all fine for musical development if they sing good music. Much of the time, unfortunately, is spent on inferior music. There is an unlimited fine literature for all of these vocal groups; and yet the average director selects some silly novelties on the ground that the public likes it. The public does like it; but the public also likes good music, effectively performed, as evidenced by the repertories of the most popular choral groups. There is no excuse for the low level of music performed by church choirs and school choruses. It indicates inertia or lack of musical ability in the director. This condition will change only when parents protest or refuse to cooperate.

Contests

Sooner or later the child who can perform fairly well, either individually or in a group, receives an invitation to enter a music contest. These contests are usually fun, since they mean a trip out of the city and offer a change from school routine. They are a help musically, because they encourage intensive practice in preparation. However, this is also one of the arguments against the contests; they concentrate so much time on one or two pieces that the organization does not have time for anything else, and musical learning is dwarfed. On this account, many school music directors are opposed to the contests and participate only to meet the demands of the school administrators.

The chief criticism of the music contests is that they are not fair. Because of the nature of music and the diversity of standards it is impossible to arrive at a rating fair to all contestants. Music has no single measure of achievement, like speed for runners or height for jumpers. A music contest is rather like a jumping contest in which some jumpers aim for height, others for distance, others for speed, and still others for good form; where neither contestants nor judges are in agreement as to what the objective really is, and where there are no ways of measuring even height or distance. The award in such a contest largely depends on chance—the predilection of the judges. Statistical studies bear this out. It is wrong to allow children to enter such contests, regardless of the high caliber of the judges, since the children inevitably think they are really going to have a fair chance. Their fate, however, hangs upon the chance of whether or not the judge selected happens to be of the same aesthetic philosophy as the child's teacher. Since most of the contestants cannot win, the odds are against a happy outcome.

Festivals

Much finer are the big music festivals that are replacing contests in the more progressive school districts. These bring together many choruses and orchestras and bands in friendly cooperation. They result in some of the finest music programs ever heard in public school programing. Church choirs sometimes organize the same type of festival service. These provide a rare musical experience for all the participants. The parent should do all he can to encourage them.

HOW CAN THE PARENT HELP

Avoid too great interest in the contests.

Encourage small groups to play in the home.

XIX

musical hobbies

MUSIC IS A HOBBY FOR MOST OF US. BUT THERE are activities associated with music which may contribute to music interest but are not actual music themselves.

Making instruments

One of the most unusual is the making of instruments. In some schools children are taught or encouraged to make instruments. In the early grades they gather stones and arrange them in order according to the pitch they sound when struck like a xylophone. They fill glasses with different amounts of water and thus construct the major scale. They string rubberbands over hollow boxes and get an instrument which can be plucked like a zither. In the upper grades they construct playable violins or complete marimbas made out of hardwood sticks and resonators. Such activities are sometimes carried on as adult avocations. Pipe organs are built in the home and fiddles and cellos are built and repaired on almost a professional scale. This is good recreation and often stimulates a genuine interest in music.

Among the children those in the primary grades thus get their first training to detect differences of pitch and to discriminate between consonance and dissonance. With the older children who construct instruments, the interest is in handicraft and physics rather than in music. It is surprising how efficient some of these instruments are.

Composition

A more musical hobby is composition. Perhaps it should not be called a hobby but rather a major musical interest. Certain it is that proficiency on an instrument often is acquired for the sake of composing. Conservative music teachers frown upon composition until a student is advanced and mature. It should be apparent to any modern educator, however, that musical composition bears the same relation to performance on an instrument that writing bears to language. They do not have to be learned together; but there is an advantage in doing so and it is unprofitable only where the teacher is not competent to carry on the instruction. Indeed, most of the great composers seem to have begun to compose at a very early age.

It would seem stupid, wouldn't it, to restrict a child learning to talk, to the vocabulary and the images supplied by the teacher? Yet this is what we traditionally do in music. Many interested parents not only encourage their children to make tunes at the piano, but take them down in notation. The same can be done on any other instrument or with the voice.

Theory

Closely related to composition are formal studies taken up by advanced students when they reach high school or college age. Among these are *form analysis, harmonic analysis, keyboard harmony, improvisation*, and *harmony* and *counterpoint*. At the earlier ages these are more or less hobbies, sometimes with little apparent relation to the music lessons. But they are all a part of music and no possible harm can come of the child's investigating them by himself. At least he will be in a better position to see the significance of such studies, when he does take them up formally. In the meantime, they are bound to have a good effect on his playing.

Record collection

The record collection is a hobby which is rapidly growing in popularity. It is surprising to hear high-school youngsters discussing the merits and demerits of the various interpretations of a symphony as played by different conductors. Even discounting the mere collector's interest, the keen listening it involves cannot help but increase appreciation of music. The hobby may appear an expensive one; but if the alternative cost of gasoline, movies, and other entertainment is weighed against the cost of the recordings, it will be found that there is very little, if any, difference in expense. Moreover, the record collection is a continuing value, often carried over into adult life, which is more than can be said of some of the other diversions.

The parent can encourage this hobby by establishing a "want" list of the recordings that the children would like as birthday or Christmas presents. Also, children enjoy owning the scores to their favorites among orchestral works. They are generally able to follow them enough to enjoy them and learn something more about their prized recordings. Some scores can be procured which have arrows to help the reader in following the themes and analyzing the composition. The best encouragement, however, comes from the parents' enjoying the recordings with their children. Radio and television are, of course, variations of this same interest. But the possession of a good recording somehow makes the music one's own. A parent whose child adopts this hobby is lucky indeed!

Children are not all alike. There is no one approach to music that is best for all. The child's hobbies are a good indication of the best way for him to learn music.

HOW CAN THE PARENT HELP

Get a jig saw, which costs about twenty dollars, and some lumber or veneer panels, out of which the child can cut his instruments.

There are books on how to make instruments. Consult them.

Listen to and comment on any compositions which the child may produce. Is the sequence always the same or does he change and develop the tune?

Buy recordings for him.

Encourage him to have a list of records that he would like to have. It is convenient for birthdays and Christmas.

Buy scores.

Listen to his records. Ask for your favorites to be played and discuss them with him.

XX

the nature of music

Cul-
ture

CULTURE INCLUDES MANY THINGS. IT IS NOT THE same for everyone. Regardless of exactly what we mean by it, its most important feature is organization—organization of ideas, of feelings, of attitudes. At college, culture is attained by organizing our knowledge of the world, in scientific studies. In the literature courses, we organize our knowledge about people and the way they behave. High schools, and even the grade schools, are concerned with the beginnings of this organization of knowledge and experience. Even more important than such organization of our knowledge of people and the world is organization of the emotions through daily experience with music and the other arts.

In music differences in taste depend upon varying ability to enjoy and respond to the elements which make up music—melody, polyphony, harmony, rhythm, tone color, tempo, dynamics, and form.

Melody

Thus the person who is sensitive to *melody* will enjoy Tschaikowsky and Schubert and Johann Strauss and other composers whose works are predominantly melodic. To be sure, there are different varieties of melody, and a person may care for only certain types. Such preferences are the result of experience or training in music. A person brought up on the conservative melodies of the old church tunes will be distressed with the chromatic vagaries of Wagner. The variety of music offered today makes great demands upon our tolerance and comprehension.

Polyphony

Most people find little difficulty in following one melody, but when asked to follow two or more melodies together, a musical form called *polyphony*, they feel frustrated. *Polyphony*, however, was one of the first developments in musical construction. We find it in obbligatos or countermelodies. It is the most important factor in the Bach fugues, the oratorios of Handel, and in chamber music. It is vital in the operas of Wagner, in the symphonies of Brahms, and in all the works of Franck. Indeed there is scarcely a masterwork which does not depend heavily upon polyphony. Nevertheless, many people are completely insensitive to it or gain only a glimmering impression from it. This is why so many do not like Bach. And people who enjoy the melody in the Franck symphony are barred from an appreciation of its real greatness by their inability to respond to its polyphony.

Harmony

Harmony is the effect made by the chords one hears—or fails to hear—beneath melodies. At the university we sometimes give the students a test in chords. Some are able to play back long series of the chords in Beethoven, Brahms, and Wagner. Others can only recall the chords which color modern jazz. Their vocabulary of chords varies with the type of music they have heard and played, just as their vocabulary in speech is dependent upon the English they have heard and the books they have read. Even advanced music students may be illiterate in harmony. As a result, music dependent upon harmony seldom has a wide appeal. As a people we Americans have not learned to organize tones into harmonic patterns.

Rhythm

Quite different is our reaction to *rhythm.* There is very little in the rhythm of the classics which escapes the modern youngster, familiar as he is with the complex and energetic patterns of present-day popular music. Rhythm is a pattern of beats, and this organization of music appeals strongly to young America. There often is difficulty in playing the rhythms, but this does not interfere with their enjoyment when someone else plays them.

Tone color

Another youthful enthusiasm of today is *tone color*—the quality or timbre of the music, which varies from instrument to instrument and from voice to voice. Each popular band which plays over the radio has its peculiar tone color, and this determines which the young people will choose as their favorite band.

The discouraging feature of tone color is that our preferences are the product of habit. My daughter's voice is more beautiful than your daughter's voice. So think I, but you will not agree. The choral conductor seeks a specific tone color for his organization and finds every other choral organization inferior in this respect. Members of choral organizations are loyal to their own conductor's concept of tone color.

The clear, unwavering tone of the flute was the orchestral ideal before 1920; any vibrato in this tone was considered an abomination. Today exactly the opposite is true. No one can prove that his ideal is best. The constant evolution of taste in tone color makes it a fascinating aspect of music.

Tempo

The variations of fast and slow, which we call *tempo*, are omnipresent in life and have the same significance in music as in speech or walking or motion of any sort. The response to tempo is universal and does not have to be learned in connection with music. The performer, however, does have to learn to control the tempo and arrange it according to the specifications of the composer. Learning to control the tempo in music develops the ability to control other emotional expression and is one of the refining powers of music.

The same is true of changes of loud and soft,

Dynamics

which we call *dynamics*. Their significance and the response to them is universal. The performer must learn to control and manipulate them. They help to emphasize the arrangement of the various elements of music and thus bring out the form or organization of the musical material.

Form

This organization, arrangement, or *form* of music is the most important of all of its elements. We enjoy the repetitions of melody and harmony. When the rhythms are repeated again and again, they become increasingly effective. It is the arrangement of the details that makes the phrases interesting, and it is the arrangement of the total mass of material that makes the great symphony a masterwork.

This is popularly believed to be the *intellectual* factor in music; but actually the form must be *felt* to be enjoyed. To take a simple instance, the melody in the first phrase of *America*, "My country, 'tis of thee," is balanced by a similar melody in the next phrase, "Sweet land of liberty." Similarly the phrase, "Land where our fathers died," is balanced by "Land of the Pilgrims' pride," and the two phrases together balance the first two. The reader can easily work out many other relations of form in this simple verse. But such analysis will not make him enjoy the song more, because he has *felt* the form long before he attempted to discover it intellectually. The value of the song came from the feeling.

The same is true of the smaller relations in a

big symphony; we *feel* them without any intellectual effort on our part. And if we wait long enough and hear the symphony enough times, we shall probably hear and feel almost all of these relationships; the program notes which analyze and call our attention to the form merely hasten the process.

A totally deaf person can *comprehend* the form of a piece of music, if it is explained to him; yet it can have no musical value for him. But when we hear the first section of a symphony come thundering back again ten minutes later and feel the comfortable resolution of the many conflicting developments in between, we *feel* the form of the composition, and no one needs to tell us about it. Since the great masterworks depend so much upon their huge and complex structure, this aspect of music is the most challenging of all. Feeling the interrelationship of the many emotional elements in a great masterwork is the very essence of musical culture.

Individual differences

All appreciation of music is limited and varied by one's response to these several elements of music. Different composers stress different elements. And people respond differently to one or another of these elements of music. This difference of response accounts for the differences in our enjoyment of music. The purpose of music lessons is to enable us to respond to all the elements of music as the composers use them.

Much of our reaction to music is due to the as-

Program music

sociations we have formed between certain musical sounds and certain experiences of life. A particular tone quality may be distantly associated with the sound of our mother's voice when we were very young or with certain speech sounds. Program music which tries to tell stories in music makes extensive use of direct association. The storm in Beethoven's *Pastoral Symphony*, and *On the Trail*, from Ferdie Grofe's *Grand Canyon Suite*, are notable examples of this type of program music. Imitative or associative power is present to some degree in almost all music.

Abstract music

At the other extreme we have music which minimizes such association and seeks to be completely abstract—pure design in sound. Such music is given no title except *sonata* or *symphony* or *fugue* or *etude*. We enjoy this music as we enjoy the design in a fine oriental rug or a colonial coverlet. The well-balanced arrangement of materials has the same ennobling effect upon us that fine architecture or perfectly spoken English has. Our emotions respond to the form in music as our mind responds to the logic in mathematics or other sciences. Some people enjoy the intellectual exercises of tracing out these abstract forms in music. Most listeners are happiest when they enjoy the feeling of just-rightness that comes with a well-constructed composition. Such ability to organize one's personal responses makes the cultured man.

A certain amount of this arrangement of musical

Indoctrination

materials is arbitrary, just as the meaning of our words is arbitrary. We may refer to our home as *a house* or *ein Haus* or *chez nous*; we can teach a child to use any one of the languages. In the same way, we can teach a child that a certain chord is dissonant or that it sounds placid.

When the beginning piano student persists in playing F-natural in a key that calls for F-sharp, it does not indicate that he is unmusical; he merely has not been indoctrinated with the etiquette of that particular scale. Such indoctrination eventually gives us a bias and we dislike music which does not conform to it. Thus parents often dislike modern music which enchants the ears of their children. There is nothing wrong with the music; it is simply using a different vocabulary. The composer arbitrarily chooses his materials of expression.

Familiarity

It follows, then, that familiarity is a great factor in the enjoyment of music. Not only does a particular composition become more enjoyable with each repeated hearing up to a point—but the harmonic progressions and the melodic patterns and the rhythmic groupings become a comfortable vocabulary to us. We enjoy new music composed of these elements.

Repetition

On the other hand, on repetition some music annoys us. This is because there is not enough substance in the piece to maintain our interest and it bores us. This is particularly true of popular music, which usually depends for its popularity upon some superficial idiom. Its vogue is like that of a slang expression which is the "rage" for a few weeks and is then dropped for another. For the same reason some overworked early classics are now considered trite. Thus the rondos of Haydn and Mozart are not often performed and are sometimes abbreviated when used. Even as modern a piece as Ravel's *Bolero* is banal to those who are not interested in orchestral variations.

Variety of taste

Sometimes a youngster seems to take a fanatical delight in playing over and over some piece that bores the rest of the family. Obviously he has come upon some source of enjoyment missed by the others. Sometimes it is merely a muscular pleasure. At other times it is the intellectual pleasure of figuring out the chord patterns. The pleasure of performing music includes much more than the pleasure of listening.

Just as people may take pleasure in one element of music while ignoring another, so a teacher may stress one element to the exclusion of some others. This is not necessarily bad teaching; some peculiarity of the pupil may demand it. But the resulting indifference of the child to certain aspects of music may distress the parent. The wise teacher determines the point of emphasis by what the pupil needs rather than by what the music requires.

However, music remains a unified experience. We do not need to dissect it to enjoy it. Our final objective in any musical study is to be able to receive the same emotional feeling or emotional impression that the composer had. That was his aim, too. The best of culture is such communication, at a high level, between the creative artist and the audience.

INDEX